Hungry for Change

My story

Amy Lewis

For
       Evie
       Emma
       Shannon
       Chloe
       Nicole
       Adele
       Hannah
       Matt
       Izzie
       Nisha

       Nina
       HolyCross College
       My family
       My friends
       Hospital staff

Thank you from the bottom of my heart for all your help and support through such a hard time.
x

A true story …

9th March 2012

    I can't believe it was 3 years ago today that I was admitted to hospital for the treatment of my eating disorder, Anorexia Nervosa. Looking back, it seems so close, but when I think about it, the painful months that lead up to discharge dragged like hell.

    A year ago last night, I didn't sleep; I didn't get into bed even, because I was up all that day and night trying to do my hair! I know this probably sounds really strange to you, but for me it was normal, a daily living nightmare. 'OCD': 'Obsessive Compulsive Disorder'. It controlled me- the way I felt, behaved, slept and ate. OCD is commonly associated with obsessive cleaning and washing of the hands, however, my obsession was different. It was with my hair. I'd awake early in the mornings, (or late at night as most people would call it), at 4am in order to sneak downstairs to have a slice of melon and a glass of orange juice as my excuse for a breakfast, and to ensure I had enough time to do my hair before setting off to college at ten to eight. I'd kneel in front of my mirror and hate what I saw in its reflection. I tried and tried to make myself look acceptable, but I just couldn't, and I despised myself.

    "Why do you have to be so ugly, you bloody weirdo?"
My hair was always tied exactly the same, day and night: a little hair tied up at each side, a little on top and a bobble at the back to tie all the pieces together! I'd redo, redo and redo my elastic bands, trying to make it look right. To 'ordinary' people it looked the same all the time, but to me, even the slightest hair that was out of place made me look like a completely different person and this made me really angry. Because I spent so much time staring at and criticising myself, I kept finding new things that were wrong with me: my nose was bent and crooked, my hair was messy and what was worse- I was fat. The scales said the opposite.

    "You're very ill", my doctor told me, "dangerously thin." But to me they were lying. Everyone was.

    College was extremely important to me. I loved what I studied: art, graphics and English, and I worked really hard. I always got good grades and would only settle for the best of my ability. The stress became overwhelming though, when I found I couldn't bring myself to do my homework, as I'd spend all day, or however long it took for me to 'look right', on my hair. I'd do nothing else and I'd greatly restrict what I ate, as I felt I didn't deserve anything. I punished myself for giving into my hunger and took it out on myself for ignoring my work for my hair, but I couldn't get way from the mirror until I was satisfied.

I'd had therapy a year before with 'Cahms': Child and Family Services, for my OCD, and it was there I was diagnosed with Anorexia. I'd dread being weighed every week; the numbers had to decrease or I'd starve myself further. Losing weight was my way of feeling pretty; in my mind, the thinner I got the better I would look. Things came to a head though at a Cahms meeting one morning where an extra supervising medical staff attended. They weighed me. Yet again I'd lost more weight. My BMI, (Body Mass Index), was now around 14.5. The average BMI for a young female adult is between 20 and 25; the lowest acceptable weight being BMI 18. I was told that if I hadn't gained 1kg by the next week's appointment, they would immediately admit me to an in-patient's eating disorder unit. I was horrified. I'd heard about those places; they weren't pleasant. They'd feed me up until I blew up like a balloon. This scared me from returning to their services and I didn't attend again.

I was on my own now- me and Anorexia. The situation worsened: I was becoming increasingly late for college; I'd feel constantly weak and tired, (enough to fall asleep in class), and I'd start screaming at the top of my voice, banging on my wardrobe doors in fits of frustration with my hair. I was breaking the family apart. We had such a close family and what had always kept me going were the happy memories from past family celebrations and holidays. Now we were arguing all the time, shouting at each other. I was frightening my little seven year old sister, Brooke- she didn't know what was going on. What was happening to her big sister? And not to mention her godmother! I was ashamed to behave this way in front of her, but I couldn't help it- aggression got the better of me and I couldn't control myself anymore. What had I become?

My mum and dad were obviously very worried about me and so one day in the car, my mum suggested trying hypnotherapy: Neurolinguistic programming, to sort out my OCD and my fear of food. My grandma, a couple of years back, had the therapy to stop her from smoking, and it worked. It must have been powerful treatment, as my grandma and cigarettes were like a dog and its bone: inseparable! The therapy cost my parents an arm and a leg, but price didn't matter as long as they could get their daughter back. I began going to sessions one evening a week. They lasted an hour and a half and explored all my emotions. At first I had no hope in the process, but I was helpless and was desperate for help, (for my OCD that is). I didn't want to let go of my fear of food. My anorexia kept me thin and was the one thing I had to feel really good about myself. The therapy would only work if I wanted it to, and so I continued to deteriorate. I was given hypnotic CDs to play every night to help positive messages sink into my subconscious. These were supposed to make me feel better about myself, and they did at first, but as I lost more and more weight, the negative thoughts dominated my mind.

The biggest warning sign that alerted me that I wasn't well was when my teachers at college began to raise their concerns about my appearance. I'd started frequently falling asleep in class and developed a gaunt tinge. They told me I needed help and hospital was the best place. Deep down I knew I needed help, but I wouldn't admit it, as that meant gaining weight; getting even uglier. For a few months I ignored their advice, until depression took over me. I'd scream and rage and slam around in my room, flinging my brush into the wall. I'd then throw myself into bed, deep down beneath the covers, and cry myself to sleep. But this didn't solve the problem- it was still there when I woke up.

"Why can't I just die? Everyone would be better off without me."

The last sign that convinced me to listen to my teachers and to seek help was the yellowy-orange patch that kept appearing on my cheek and around my mouth. I was really worried about it and made me even more paranoid about the way I looked. I decided to get it checked out with the GP: The results of the blood tests confirmed I had developed liver problems and I knew why: lack of food.

The following week at college, I had a long chat with my teachers about what to do. There was only one option- I was going to have to go to hospital. I went home and told my mum the hardest thing I've ever had to tell her: that I needed help and I wanted her to take me to hospital. When I'd told her, a huge weight felt as though it had been lifted from my shoulders- my health was going to be monitored now- I no longer had to worry about myself on my own. Although, my anorexia gave me a hard time for this,

"You stupid, stupid girl. What have you done? You know what will happen now don't you? You're going to get fat!"

I began to wonder if I'd done the right thing. Over the following few nights whilst my mum contacted the hospital, I lay in bed flat on my back and ran my hands along my hips and my ribs; all the bones that jutted out at pointy angles and said goodbye to the features that made me proud of my body. When we informed college about the hospital, they were brilliant. They were so understanding and even guaranteed me an extra year there when I recovered to come back and complete my A levels. This meant so much to me. It meant my mind could relax and concentrate on sorting myself out. The head teacher, Mr. David Frost, also offered me extra support and took time out from his busy schedule to sit and chat with me about an ex-student he'd taught at another school who had been through exactly what I was going through now. Judith Fathallah was her name and she'd written and published a book about her experiences, "Monkey Taming". She'd signed him a copy and he leant it to me for as long as a needed it. It was great to read about someone else like me. Who would have thought of it? Another human being, just like me!

"What do you want to do that for? You're ill- a proper anorexic; I'm proud of you for that."

I had to have blood tests and blood pressure taken every day at hospital for two weeks to make sure the levels in my blood weren't becoming dangerous in any way. And then we got the call. The next day, my parents and I were going to look around the hospital and I was to be assessed by the nurses.

Driving there through "Hill Top" in Altrincham, where the footballers lived, I gawped at the grandness of the area and hoped the hospital was as nice as its surroundings. It was nice: beautiful in fact, but when my dad pulled up the long drive and I saw the hospital for real, my stomach turned and I just wanted to go back and run as fast as I could.

"Mummy, I've changed my mind, take me home I don't want to go to hospital anymore."

"It's too late, we're here now and it's what you need."

I clutched onto my mum, linking her arm in arm as we walked through the hooded walkway towards the main reception. It was then that the woman I'd hate for the next seven months, but be grateful for at the end of my admission, strode down the staircase. She introduced herself as Dr.Waissel- the doctor in charged of the eating disorders patients- and led us to the ward.

It was in the middle of refurbishment- two more beds had been added. Now it bedded eight patients. Was one of those beds mine? Fay, one of the nurses and ward manager, gave us a tour of the unit. It was lovely and warm, covered in colourful artwork from patients and lit with colour-changing spotlights. The atmosphere was dampened though, when I peered into a room labeled with a splodgy painted sign, the "Dining Room". A group of skinny, skinny girls with gaunt faces that resembled death sat at a long glass table dotted with staff and stared like frightened kittens at food on plates in front of them. They glanced up through sunken eyes out of black sockets and I disappeared into a side room with my family and Fay.

A second woman, quiet and friendly, came in shortly after and sat opposite me. She was Eliza, one of the ward's psychologists. They wanted to talk to my parents on their own first, so they sent me to the neighbouring room with magazines and newspapers. About ten minutes passed and they called me back in. It was my turn to speak and my feelings just flooded out.

"I just don't know how to cope anymore, I'm so confused and I hate myself. I need help but I don't know what's wrong with me." I choked through the sobbing. I just cried and cried whilst I told them everything. All my problems poured out of me like water bursting through a dam. Part of me regretted confessing all these feelings- I didn't want them to take my thinness away from me.

"You've said enough. Stop before it's too late."

The nurses listened with crinkled brows in silence, and I just wondered if they thought I was strange. At the end of the assessment, they lead me to the 'treatment room' to get weighed. I hated this; they would see my weight and know I wasn't thin enough to pass as a 'poorly anorexic'. On the way out, the group of thin girls that had been gathered in the dining room walked past and my eyes just stared in disbelief and jealousy at their skinny bodies. A couple ushered me a friendly smile, whilst others glanced sadly at me and continued by, eyes on the floor. Now I knew I wasn't worthy of being there. They were *way* thinner than I was...or so I thought.

Two days later, the hospital rang to confirm my admission the following day. I went into college and my art teacher, Ms.Elliott, wished me all the best and gave me a big hug. I'd miss her so much. She'd taken out so much time to talk to me and look after me after hours. I left the college building knowing that I'd never tread on its floors the same weight again. That evening, I went round to Ramsbottom's local artist's house, Barry Tomlinson, who also happened to be my art teacher for the past nine years. My little sister and nana had made a box full of home made cakes for him. We'd recently found out he had chronic lung cancer and would not be able to be cured. A few weeks before, me and four other students agreed to bake him lots of treats to make him feel better, as he loved his cakes! As I was going into hospital, I wouldn't be able to give him mine with the others, and so I thought I'd take them round early. I couldn't help filling up when I entered his home. I had that haunting feeling that I'd never see or have another art class with him again. However, when he answered the door, he looked much perkier than he had looked the last time I'd seen him; he had colour in his cheeks and he had a spring in his walk again. This settled my mind slightly and I hoped he'd be okay. I gave him a massive squeeze and left.

That night I didn't go to bed. It was the longest night I've ever had to endure. There were so many thoughts circling in my head and my only coping strategy was to retreat to my mirror and start rearranging my elastic bands: hating myself more with every second that passed. When morning crept in and my room lightened, I was still crouched on my floor, with red knees and black caves engulfing my exhausted eyes. I still hadn't got it right, I still looked uglier than ever and no way did I deserve food for being so hideous. We had to be ready and packed to leave the house at half past one to travel to the hospital, and I hadn't even packed a thing. Whilst my dad went to work and my brother and sister had gone to school, my mum went out somewhere; she didn't say where. I just continued to mess with my hair. When my mum returned I heard a rustle of bags. She shouted me down, so I left my hair, just for a minute, as I'd had enough of this palaver. I sauntered down the stairs clutching my dressing gown which was tied round my waist and she gave me lots of presents for my new hospital room: An alarm clock, a clock radio, sentimental gifts to hang in my room that had special words engraved on them, 'You are a very special person…just wanted to make sure you always remember that', and brand new toiletries, including a shiny red and silver toilet brush for my bathroom! My eyes swelled full of tears and I hugged her tight.

"You are going to get better and the Amy we all know is going to come back. I love you so much and everyone is here to support you." These words comforted me and drew us even closer than we already were. To distract me from returning to my obsessive rituals, we made a cup of tea and sat in the lounge to watch one of my favourite programmes, "Supersize vs. Super skinny". I filled with envy as the super skinny girl emerged on the screen- why wasn't she being taken to a hospital to be fed? And I winced at the gross size of the supersize girl.

"That's what they're going to do to you. There's no escaping this now."

When it had finished I returned upstairs with the intention to get dressed and pack my things, however, the mirror was taunting me and pulled me back to its cruel tormenting.

"Oh you ugly sod, why? Why?" Eventually though, in dribs and drabs, I managed to get my clothes on and scribble a list of everything I needed to take with me. I crammed my belongings into two large plastic crates and ran downstairs in desperate need for food. I wanted something, but it had to be mega healthy; something that hardly had any calorific content: lettuce, cherry tomatoes, and cucumber and mini sweet corns. I ate this quickly so my mum didn't see how little I was eating and yet again returned upstairs to my mirror out of guilt for eating. I had ten minutes before we left and I'd untied my hair and started again! My dad's car prowled up the drive- he was home early from work to take us to the hospital. In the last pressured minutes, I tied my bobbles quickly and untidily in an effort to be ready for my parents. Whilst my dad loaded the car with all my things, I stood in front of the mirror, gripping my freshly filled hot water bottle and stared in disgust at the ugly, dying figure I saw before me. I started to cry and I reluctantly said goodbye to my room.

As I took my last step in my house before exiting, all my emotions churned in my tummy and I felt physically sick. I blew a kiss goodbye to my house and perched myself into the backseat of the car.

"This is a fresh start, Amy", my dad reassured. "When you step back in our house you'll be a happy person again, just look at it that way." I stared down at my legs- they were fat slugs and I just wished I wasn't there.

"I'll be happier, won't I mummy? When I come back? I'll feel like I used to and not bother about my hair, like a normal person?"

"Of course you will. All the nurses are there to look after you and make you better." But I wasn't convinced. How could this controlling nightmare possibly leave me alone? It had been haunting me for as long as I could remember.

As 'Hill Top' emerged ahead, fear took over and I squeezed my hot water bottle for extra comfort. I could just about see the top of the hospital's building over the surrounding tall hedges and trees. I think this was one of the few times I'd turned to God for help: I prayed and prayed for him to help me and to keep me thin. There was nothing else I could do. My dad pulled into the car park and I was reluctant to get out of the car, and anyway, the car park was full, yes! But there was no turning back. Whilst my mum took me, hand in hand, towards the ward, my dad went and parked elsewhere.

A short, jolly woman with a broad Birmingham 'twang' to her voice welcomed us into the ward. She introduced herself as Moira, my named nurse who would look after my care plan, and led us to that side room, (the community room), where Fay saw me for my assessment. I was in such a depressed state: my hair was a mess and wasn't how I wanted it; I was ugly and fat and I was there to become even fatter! What was the point of living? This was all on top of the fact that I was completely exhausted from having no sleep and virtually no food. I just sat nervously on the edge of a chair, clutching my coat in front of me as to hide my body shape, and held my mummy's hand. Moira took about half an hour to ask loads of pointless questions, like, "With who do you currently live?" What was the bloody relevance of that? I was there to get help, not interrogated about my whereabouts! My dad, who had joined us ten minutes into the 'interrogation', sat jovially with a happy expression on his face, which just said to me that he was happy about getting some 'meat' on me. But I guess he was just thankful and relieved I was in good hands. A nursing assistant entered with a menu and asked me what I'd like for tea. 'Nothing', I wanted to say, but didn't. He read me the options and I chose the healthiest sounding one, "Mushroom Provencal", which probably had the least calories in it.

Next stop was the treatment room and I got on the scales: 32.1kg. I'd lost weight from just three days ago. This made me feel really good. This was an achievement and I was proud of this tiny measurement. I was then shown to my room where I'd spend the majority of my time over the next seven months. I've got to hand it to them, it was beautiful: Lovely oak draws and shelves; a single bed loaded with cushions; a leather armchair; a huge wooden desk, perfect for doing my artwork which I adored, and an en suite - complete with a bath and a built in shower. And if this wasn't enough, it overlooked the ward's large garden and blossoming magnolia tree, which touched my window with its branches. But most importantly, a large mirror loomed above my desk which was essential for my hair routines. However, this did not budge my mood. It didn't dissolve the fact that I was in there to get fatter.

The doctor assessed me next. His voice was funny. He was Polish. I had to ask him to repeat each question at least twice for me to understand. My mum and I exchanged bemused glances. Next in was the dietician; she asked me what foods I liked and disliked. In my mind my lists would have looked something like this:

	Like
Dislike	
	Water
Cheese	
	Fruit
Butter	
	Vegetables
Bread	
Milk	

Cereal
Chocolate…basically anything stodgy or calorific.

It wasn't that I didn't *like* the food, I just wouldn't allow myself to eat it. Although, I was only allowed three dislikes, as apparently part of the illness tells you false information which I end up believing. So I chose butter, cheese and chocolate as my three dislikes. She could now write a diet plan for me.

Shortly after she left, my mum and dad moved my stuff in to my room- everything but the kitchen sink! As a last surprise, my mum lifted a fluffy pink teddy from the suitcase which wore a t-shirt embroidered with the words, 'AMY'S GET WELL BEAR LOVE YOU SO MUCH xxxxxxxxxxxx', and a velvety pink cushion embroidered with the message, 'Hug Me Every Day And I Will Be With You Love Mummy xx'. I squeezed the cushion, the teddy and my mum really tight and filled up with tears. It was now ten to five and a nursing assistant came to fetch me for tea. This was it. My treatment had begun. I turned to my mum and the tears came flooding out. Her eyes were red and puffy too; I knew she wanted to cry but was holding it in as not to upset me. I threw my arms around her and never wanted to let go. We were so close- best friends and I'd never been separated from her or daddy before. I hugged and kissed my parents goodbye as I got ushered into the dining room. Now I was 'full-on' crying, hard.

"Mummy, don't go, mummy I love you. Take me home mummy." The group of skinny girls I'd met the other day strolled past; tension pasted upon their faces. One patient, Sharon, who had a tube up her nose, smiled at me and took my hand.

"You'll be okay, come with me." She led me away from my family into the dining room.

Still sobbing, I sat at the head of the table. I felt really embarrassed and out of place and felt as though everyone was turning their eyes to look at me. And what made things ten times worse was having a glass table. You could see straight through it, right down to your fat legs and so I didn't know how to position them. My tea lay in front of me on a plate fastened tight with cling film. I was actually really hungry as I'd hardly eaten anything, but was unsure whether it was normal or acceptable to eat without a reaction, being anorexic.

It was red mush dotted with mushrooms, green vegetables and sliced potatoes that looked fried in something greasy. I started with the veg, (as I'd gladly eat this food group), and forked out the mushrooms lingering in the sauce. Once I'd eaten what I'd allowed myself, I placed my knife and fork, one on top of the other, on my plate to show I'd finished.

I had not finished.

The nurses told me that it was 'the rules' to eat EVERYTHING that was put in front of me. I looked reluctantly at the greasy lumps on the plate. Then I stopped.

"Even the potatoes?" I asked.

"Yes, everything", one of the nurses replied.

"All of them?" I wanted to know. She nodded. After the main course my pudding was an apple, so at least that was safe to have. I asked to leave the table, but the nurse told me that I had to sit there for half an hour's supervision after every meal and snack. I mean, honestly, what was I going to do? Throw it all back up? Exercise? That's just not what I did. It wasn't my way. They weren't to know that though were they?

Finally half an hour was up and I couldn't wait to get back to my room. I shut myself in and started to unpack. I blue-tacked Mickey mouse posters and photos of my family along the walls and shelves to remind me of home and all the good things. I kissed each picture as I stuck it up and began to sob again, clutching my teddy.

A faint knock on the door broke the sobbing. I told them to come in. It was Sharon; she'd brought me a homemade card and a friendship bracelet. This meant so much to me.

Amy ♡ Shan
best friends 4eva.
xx

Keep your chin up and smile
x ☺ x

Amy

hi ☺, I hope your ok and settle in really well. You seem dead nice and I can't wait to have a good chat with you. If you ever need anything or someone to talk to am here for you all the way.
GET WELL Soon
♥ Love alwayz & forever ♥
xxx Shan xxx

"I'll be your friend, and if you ever need anything I'll be there for you hunny." Sharon offered, rubbing my arm. She plunged herself onto my chair and sat bent over with her chin in her hands.

"What you in for? Anorexia?" she asked.

"Yeah. You too?"

Yep. And bulimia. Been in here twice now. Last time I just relapsed when I went home." She declared, quite openly. This was great. Finally someone who was just like me; someone who could understand.

"It's hard, isn't it?" I gestured.

"Real hard, but you'll get through it, I know you can do it." She reassured.

"Ahh, thanks", I said as I leaned to give her a big hug. However, my mind was thinking something rather different; I didn't want to get better. I liked the weight I was and was absolutely adamant that no one could do anything to change it. I didn't want to be able to 'get through it'. A nurse opened my bedroom door and told Sharon to get out, as it was against the rules to be in each other's rooms. About an hour later another, fainter knock tapped at my door. I opened it and there stood a beautiful young girl in her dressing gown. She had dark brown hair, olive skin and huge brown eyes staring back at me. Her name was Ellie, but it was the tube that I noticed before anything else. It went up her nose and was taped to her cheek.

"Hi!" She said through a big smile.

"Hi, I'm Amy." I said smiling.

"I'm Ellie." She gave me a shy hug and swiftly left. 'Well, at least the girls are friendly', I thought. That was a start.

As I got ready to get changed for bed, I was summoned, yet again, to the dining room. What? Breakfast? Already? Nope: supper. This was a meal in between tea and breakfast. I really didn't want anything else to eat.

After supervision, the patient pay phone rang. It was for me: my mum. My eyes lit up for the first time in a long while. Just the familiar, sweet sound of my mum's voice was enough to relax my tense muscles and produce goose-bumps down both my arms and my back.

"Mummy!" I cried. "I love you, I want to come home. Please mummy!"

I began to cry.

"Amy, Amy, it's okay", she reassured, "don't cry." But I missed her so much.

"And I miss you too, but this is the best place for you. You need help and the nurses there can help you be happy again."

"You promise?" I asked, doubtfully.

"Yes." She replied, and she was quick to change the subject. "What was for tea?" I described the mound of, 'what-they-called food, I had to eat, even though I was full half way through.

"Have you finished unpacking yet?"

"No, not yet. I'm going to finish it before I go to bed."

"Okay, but don't go to bed too late; you know you're getting up early." Me, my mum and Dr.Waissel had agreed that on my care plan, it would specifically specify that I could get up very early every morning with plenty of time to do my hair. This meant 4am on mornings when I washed my hair! There was a strict rule that all the young people must be out of their rooms and ready for half past eight in time for breakfast. In order for me to be ready, I had to be sure I had enough time. Three hours was not a long time to do my hair...well, not for me anyway. Maybe five would've been better, but they were no way on this earth allowing me to get up any earlier!

My mum's voice became fainter and slurred, as if she was choking on her own words. I could tell she was trying not to cry.

"Don't cry mummy, you'll set me off!" I said in a blubber. After our long and comforting talk on the phone, I reluctantly went back to my room to unpack.

The next morning at the breakfast table, I had a huge shock. The nursing staff placed half a portion of cereal and milk in front of me and a cup of apple juice. The juice was fine, I was used to that. It was the cereal and milk that frightened me, since I'd only been used to eating melon in the mornings for quite some time. The cereal lay dry in a bowl and the milk separate in a cup. I drank the juice then sat defiantly with my arms crossed and pushed the food away from me.

"I'm not eating that." I said and looked in the opposite direction. The nurse, Keri, gave me a look as if to say 'come on, eat it', but I shook my head and stuck to my guns.

"Just the cereal…" she offered.

Still, no.

"You're going to have to eat it." She told me.

"No." I started to cry, so she took me into the 'group room', away from the others, to finish my cereal. But I was adamant I wasn't going to finish. After about fifteen minutes of persuading me to eat it, I took small spoonfuls: one at a time; scooping out the flakes and making sure to miss the milk.

"There are still flakes left", she pointed out. So I grabbed the spoon, swiped the last few flakes I could out of the milk, thrust the spoon into my mouth and said, "There. Okay?"

"Now the milk." She had the cheek to say. I was very upset now; tears were streaming down my face and I tucked my knees into my chest and slouched back on the chair, sobbing into my knees. She could see I was highly distressed and so a rare thing happened: she let me leave, unfinished. This was only because I was new to the place and it was my first breakfast there, which could be a daunting experience.

After, we had education. This was part of the weekly plan- five days a week, like school, Monday to Friday. Leanne, or 'Li' as she liked to be called was the teacher, and she was awesome! Her dress sense was so retro and colourful. I liked her platform shoes and mini skirts the best, and she rode a motor bike! The education room was separate to the main building and was situated just around the corner, literally a minute's walk away. I was looking forward to sinking into some artwork to take my mind off things, but when I found out I was only allowed to be taken there in a wheelchair I was miffed.

"I'm not bloody disabled you know!" I told them. But they insisted I was too ill to walk and that my organs could potentially 'pack-in' at any time. Although this alarming news worried me, I didn't believe them; besides, if I was really that ill, wouldn't doctors have admitted me to hospital months ago?

On the way over I clutched my coat and pulled my hood tight over my head in order to prevent the wind from 'ruining' my hair. I crossed my arms and legs in defiance and stared at the floor. But out of the corner of my eye, a lady, who seemed faintly familiar to me with bleach blonde hair, caught my attention. At a second glance I recognised her: it was her from behind the bar on Corrie, having a fag! She smiled down at me huddled in my wheelchair. A simple smile from a famous face made me feel really special, and I almost felt good for a second.

"Hey it's her from Corrie!" I shouted as I stared back over the top of the wheelchair, but the nurse pushing me was quick to shush me up!

Lunch was half a sandwich, apparently spread 'lightly' with margarine, and a piece of fruit. This would have been fine, apart from the bread was smothered with thick lumps of margarine. I had to get rid of these pure lumps of fat, so I discretely wiped the excess spread off with my finger and hid it in the cling film, which the meal came wrapped in. 'That's a few less calories to worry about', I thought.

There were a few times I'd gotten away with this, and it was made practically easier when I held onto a tissue, which provided a wonderful hiding place. Because it was Friday, tea was a trip to the buffet bar at 'The Grange', (the main restaurant area for staff, patients and their families.) The young people got to walk over and select what they wanted- supervised, obviously! But I wasn't allowed to walk over, 'in case I died'! This was pathetic; so whilst everyone else who was on 'solids' went over, I stayed on the unit with staff. By 'solids' I mean people who were eating actual food. Some patients chose to drink calorie shakes such as 'Scandishake', 'Fortisip' or 'Fortijuice' instead, for this made the guilt of consuming calories much less daunting, as you didn't actually have to 'eat' the food- just drink it.

I'd made another friend that day: Amber. She was a lovely girl who loved art, like me, and was a similar age too, and had bulimia. We got on like sisters and we could really relate to one another. Since I was not allowed over and she was, I asked her to choose things for me, as I trusted her not to pick anything fatty or stodgy. She chose most things alright, although I was not over excited about the potato salad she'd chosen, as it was covered in a thick mayonnaise, which I forbid myself from having.

Despite still feeling low that night on the patient pay phone, I had one thing to look forward to- the following day my mum and dad were coming to visit me in the afternoon. I didn't want my brother and sister to see me yet in case I got too upset in front of them. I couldn't wait to hold them in my arms and forget about what was happening to me. I ate my supper without a problem, as I just wanted tomorrow to come as quick as possible.

Saturday morning came and even though I was looking forward to seeing my parents, I had struggled immensely since half past five with my hair. It was now nearly half past eight and I hadn't even got dressed- never mind done my hair.

"You are so ugly it's untrue. And things are just going to get worse as you get fatter and fatter and fatter."

Carmina, a new nurse to the ward, came into my room and told me it was time for breakfast. I threw myself onto my chair and cried. She was lovely and came to comfort me, but never mind how nice she was, there was no getting me out of having more time on my hair before breakfast.

"I'm not coming for breakfast, I can't!" I told her in a flurry. I was afraid of anyone else seeing me before I managed to make myself look 'right', because then everyone else would see how ugly and fat I really was. Nobody would like me then.

"Just five minutes, please?" I begged her. That was not an option. She helped me to put my dressing gown on and took me to the dining room. When I entered, I knew everyone was looking at me. My face was stained with tears, my eyes were black and my hair was half done. I looked at nobody, just my cereal. I ate it in silence and didn't take my eyes off it once. I sat through half an hour's supervision with my face in my hands and then I left without a sound. The whole morning was spent doing my hair, but because I was at a very dangerous weight and was new, I was assessed as 'red risk' and needed to be checked on every ten minutes. This was highly annoying, as I couldn't possibly complete my OCD routines when people were interrupting them all the time. I felt so weird and awkward always being found in front of my mirror when staff opened the door to check on me, with bits of hair clasped in one hand and a brush in the other. What were they thinking? I really hoped they didn't think I was vein, as I wasn't- far, far from it; the opposite in fact. I felt pure hatred and despise and all I could do to try and sort things out was to 'fix' my ugliness. As time ticked by, and my hair still undone, my parents arrived. I was informed of their arrival, but kept them waiting just a couple more minutes so I could make myself look presentable. I wanted them to be proud of how I looked, not embarrassed. Eventually, I burst out of my room and thrust myself into my mum's arms.

"Take me home mummy; take me home, I hate it here!" I begged through the tears. My parents didn't look too impressed by their welcome, so I forced a smile onto my face and led them into the community room.

The visit went terribly. I cried through most of it, and through the parts I didn't I struggled to hold it in. I was so much closer to my mum than my dad, as his attitude was, "You're in here to gain weight and you're not coming out until you have." Whereas my mum's was that she too wanted the best for me, but also, being my mother, felt pressured into doing what I felt was best for me, which was to get them to take me out of there. So, with contrasting opinions and an awkward atmosphere, it was time for my parents to leave.

It was now half past eight: supper. I was in no mood to eat, so I refused the food. Anyway, the night staff were known to be generally 'softer' than the day staff, and so the easier it was to get away with having nothing. I went to bed knowing I'd have to make up the calories the following day.

Once the weekend past and Monday came, it was time for the dreaded 'weigh-in'. This was to happen three times a week: Monday, Wednesday and Friday mornings before breakfast. The other girls came out of their rooms and sauntered round the corner of the lounge in their dressing gowns, getting ready to exchange details and measurements and to get 'meds', (medications). I stayed in my room. I was still reluctant to join in with 'the program'. When a nurse tapped on my door and led me to the 'treatment room', I felt much fatter than the other girls as I walked along the corridor in my pyjama shorts; the other patients eyeing me up as I went; comparing bodies. I hoped they weren't saying how un-anorexic I was.

The scales loomed in the icy-cold room. I took off my dressing gown and slippers and slowly stepped onto the scales. I prayed to have stayed the same, or to have lost, but part of me knew that if this was the case, I'd surely get diet increases until I started to gain. It was a maze with a dead end... '31.2 kg'. Yes, I'd lost weight since my admission and my BMI was now 13. Fay in my assessment told me it was very common for a new patient to have lost weight in the first week- mainly down to stress. I strode confidently down the corridor back to my room with a huge grin pasted on my face.

But that grin didn't last for long. After breakfast, morning snack and education, a plate with a full sandwich, bursting with prawns and salad; cut into four triangles, was place beneath tightly wrapped cling film in front of me. I was quick to respond, "This isn't mine."

"Yes it is", the nurse assured, "you've had a diet increase." The other girls glanced at each other and smirked. They'd all been there; done that and all had to endure diet increases. Now it was my turn. My stomach churned, and not for food! All I could do was stare at the pyramids of calories.

"I am *not* eating all of that." It was off-putting, all that food, so I didn't want to attempt any of it. Instead I sat back a rocked in my chair, staring out the window. I had to endure continuous nags to eat whilst watching the painful squirms on the other girl's faces as they slowly ate or sucked up their calories through a half-chewed straw. Sharon smiled up at me from her straw and gave me a thumbs up. It was strange other people living off liquids all day, everyday. Had they always done that? But why? I was sure that I'd never retreat to liquids. I didn't know what was in them: all those unfamiliar chemicals swirling about in a cup. Did they make you put weight on any faster than solids? I was in no hurry to find out. I knew exactly what was in every type of food, (after years of memorising the labels on every packet I got my hands onto), and so there were no mysteries about how that particular food had been made.

"Come on Amy, I know you can do it", Kelly, a short, blonde nursing assistant encouraged. I was now on my own. All the other girls had left ages ago and it was getting closer and closer to afternoon snack.

"But look at the size of it- it's huge! And how many prawns did the chef have to cram in?! It's as though they want me to get fat!"

"I know it looks scary, but it's a normal portion and you have to eat it." She tried.

"Well you can't force it down my throat, that'd be child abuse", I threatened. The room fell silent.

"But the tube can." Kelly reminded me. That was the first time I'd been warned with the tube. No way was I going to allow a strange plastic tube to be passed up my nose and into my stomach, pumping god-only-knows-what into me. This threat always seemed to work though. I reached for the orange and began peeling.

"I'm only eating this though" I reiterated.

"Well, we'll start with that", she added. 'And finish with that too', I felt like saying. Ten minutes passed and I'd eaten the orange and was convinced I'd finished.

"Done." I announced. But I knew I hadn't really, and still wasn't allowed to leave until it was all gone. I tried stalling for another quarter of an hour, until I realised that this wasn't like the first breakfast where I was let off from leaving some. She was really putting her foot down. As I tugged the plate closer to me and broke off bite size pieces with my fingers, my eyes filled up, and as I took the first mouthful, shame set in.

"What are you doing? You're letting them win, you idiot."

I'd eaten half the sandwich and that was enough: no more, as that meant more than yesterday, which meant a step towards gaining weight. I refused to go any further, but there was no choice. I *had* to finish it. After a long and difficult hour of fighting with ED, (the little demon in my head telling me not to eat), and forcing bits of bread into my mouth, I had finally finished, but now had half an hour's supervision to reflect on what I'd just done to myself. As Kelly tried to distract me from this line of thought, I just couldn't ignore how much they were making me eat. (But I'd had nothing yet!)

Once supervision was up, I rushed to the phone and told my mum in disgust about my unnecessary diet increase and told her how I wasn't going to have any of it and pleaded her to take me home. Lunch wasn't the only meal to be increased. Two of my snacks had also been changed from just fruit to fruit and a yogurt. That meant two yogurts a day, and in my mind, that was not allowed. I wouldn't eat them, I wouldn't.

On Tuesday I met another nursing assistant, Abby. She came in early in the morning to take my blood pressure. Again I felt stupid, as I was perched on my desk in front of my mirror doing my hair. My blood pressure reading was really low, and so I was told to get straight back into bed in case I fainted. Consequently, breakfast was breakfast in bed, and Abby had to supervise on a chair in my room. I hated this. I felt dead lazy eating in my bed. Everyone else gathered at my door on their way down to the dining room and whispers filled the air. In a way, I enjoyed being cut off from everyone else, as it meant that I *was* ill and confirmed I *was* anorexic and so needed looking after. She took my blood pressure again a couple more times in the following hour and the readings were increasing promisingly, so she allowed me to get out of bed and get ready for education. Abby was unaware of my wheelchair situation, so I didn't say anything. Why would I? I gave the girls hard stares as if to say, 'don't you dare say a thing.' I let Abby open the door of the unit to lead the way, but not even a fifth of the way there our giggles and sniggers caught her suspicion. And to make things even more obvious, Moira was watching us from the office window and it clicked that I didn't have a wheelchair.

"No!" Moira shouted from upstairs, and with that, Abby gave me a shameful look and told us to stay there whilst she fetched a wheelchair.

"I am not amused, Amy." Abby let me know, but I was; it was good to have a laugh and make the nurse's lives difficult!

Over the following few nights, I'd noticed a rough, red mark appear on my hip and on one bottom cheek. It was quite uncomfortable, so I got the nurses to check it out. It was a pressure mark. These were areas of your body where, when there is a lot of bone, it rubs against the mattress at night. They told me of patients they'd had in the past whose pressure marks became infected and they needed to be bathed and treated every day by the nurses. I didn't want anyone else to see my chubby body, and so I agreed to sleep on an air bed, for my own safety. I liked the air bed at first. It was like you were sleeping on just air, literally! But eventually, its lethargic wheeze, as it inflated and deflated and pumped air round the bed became irritating. Its bumpy movements that made me float up and down, made me feel sick, and the shrill, high pitched bleeps that frequently sounded in the middle of the night, triggered by a default in the attached electrical box, hurt my ears. I couldn't stand it. The days were difficult enough without the unwanted intrusion invading my dreams: the only place I got to have peace and to hide myself away in my own world where I felt safe.

Every Monday, Wednesday and Friday, the whole ward held a community meeting in the community room. This was a place to let everyone else know how you are feeling, to make aims to accomplish over the week and to address any current issues that may be taking place on the ward. We decided between us who was to take each meeting. I didn't want to, as that would be participating in the program and to be perfectly honest, I was not interested. They had to ask how everyone was and write the aims down for the week. We decided Lizzie, another patient, who was very quiet, yet had a very stylish look: short, bleach-blonde layered hair and earrings pierced in cool places in her ears, should take that meeting. When it was my turn to speak, I let everyone know how low I was feeling.

"I'm doing terrible. I don't like it here and I want to go home." I wouldn't say more than that. I hoped my message had gotten across.

Groups weren't any better either. 'Support Group' was the worst. It was so depressing. Although it was a good chance to discuss the similar feelings we shared with other people and learnt to relate to one another, it was sometimes upsetting to witness one of your close friends break down in tears over their difficulties. And when it came to your turn to speak, the concentration on that particular emotion you were discussing was so strong, it was almost like re-living the moment. Oh, and nutrition group with the dietician was unbearable. I'd already learnt the tedious nutritional facts certain food groups played in the body, and didn't appreciate having to be told, again, what was good for me and what was not. Besides, I made those kinds of decisions for myself. If I changed the rules I'd set myself, I was afraid of that resulting in weight gain.

After another few days of intense emotional stress caused by continuous diet increases and OCD problems, I'd started to gain weight. I'd gained 0.7 of a kilogram in under a week: nearly two and a half pounds. This was awful.

"See, you're fatter already, and you've hardly started your treatment yet. Just you wait another couple of weeks and you'll really notice the difference. Your clothes won't fit and you'll grow another chin!"

I couldn't bare it anymore; I just had to get out of there. So one morning after snack, I gathered my coat, gloves and a bag containing stamps, writing paper, envelopes, a pen and my phone and loitered behind my door; waiting for the perfect moment to 'leg it'. Unfortunately, due to my regular ten minute checks, my plan was foiled when Geri, (a nurse on duty that day), opened my door and soon gathered what I was up to. This, I would soon discover, was the worst move I'd make during my stay at the hospital. She told me to stay-put whilst she went to find an official document of some kind and returned to my room to go through it with me. The paper was entitled, 'Section 3 of the Mental Health Act'. She explained that I should be placed on a section, which is a policy put in place to ensure my care would be carried out until I was well, and that it would be in my best interest for me to sign the slip, confirming my permission. So, being young and uneducated in this field, (and not to mention blonde), I signed it. But god-damn I soon wished that I hadn't.

I hadn't realised it at the time, but I'd just legally handed over all power over my care to the hospital and the law. This meant that they had authority over me; even over my parents: it was now illegal for them to take me out of hospital…even if they wanted to, (without a doctor's consent). And the doctor was never going to let me out until I was heavier. It was a catastrophe. And it turned out that all the other patients had been placed on the section too, so I quickly learnt that it lasts for six months. I was doomed.

There had to be a way to get free of the section so then my mum and dad could take me out of there. I did a lot of research over the following week into the different ways of going about this. There were numerous posters on the walls of the ward advertising advocates for young people who felt they had been wrongly placed on a section. I quickly learned of an official 'tribunal meeting' that could be organised to decide whether or not it was necessary for me to be under a section. I rang many numbers on my mobile, whilst I knelt nervously over my bed in my room, until one particular advocate of interest, 'Barbara', offered to come and visit me in the near future to discuss my situation further. This was great. A real chance to prove to people of importance that I am not anorexic and that I can eat properly at home without losing any more weight. And so, I had set a challenge for myself: I was going to have to 'put on a brave face' and pretend to everyone that I was doing well and coping fine with the weight gain in order to make a good reason for me to be let off my section. This meant trying not to refuse meals, showing no stress in emotions group and, most importantly…gaining weight. This, however, was the catalyst for a 'fool-proof' plan that I was about to put into action.

Meanwhile, I had in fact reached a BMI of 14 without the help of a few 'tricks of the trade', and so, as Dr. Waissel had promised, this enabled me more freedom and the privilege of being able to do more things with my family. In order for me to obtain these privileges however, I had to ask for them in my ward round requests every week. Ward round was held every Friday and was a meeting attended by Dr. Waissel, the dietician, Li the school teacher, Eliza the psychologist, the main nurse that day and a few other members as well. It was an opportunity for patients to ask for privileges, such as walks, home leave, and the permission to make your own meals or snacks and lots of other things. This was in return for progress made, and by 'progress' I mean weight gain. I wrote:

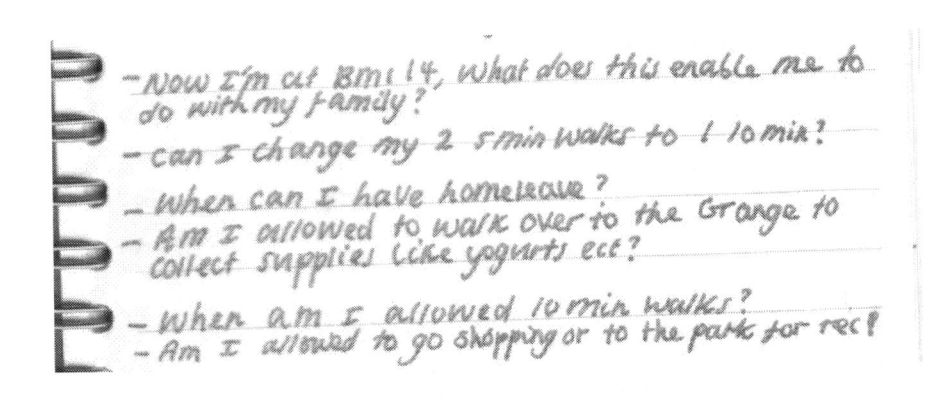

> - Now I'm at BMI 14, what does this enable me to do with my family?
> - Can I change my 2 5min walks to 1 10min?
> - When can I have home leave?
> - Am I allowed to walk over to the Grange to collect supplies like yogurts ect?
> - When am I allowed 10 min walks?
> - Am I allowed to go shopping or to the park for rec?

The top point was the one I desired most, for if I had more time with my family and less on the ward, maybe it wouldn't feel so much like a prison.

The ward round results were given in the afternoon, and the process made me feel like a naughty child being called into a principle's office. We were called one at a time and escorted by Dr.Waissel to an isolated room, where she'd sit in front of a ring binder of documents and tell us what they'd decided we deserved. It turned out that: I was allowed two five minute walks around the grounds a day; I was allowed on recreation, on the basis that I didn't walk far or did no strenuous exercise and I was allowed out for an hour's drive with my parents. As for the walking to the Grange, that was a no. But the best news was that next week, I was to have a supervised meal with my parents on the ward, and if this went successfully I'd maybe be allowed home for part of the day the following week. I couldn't wait.

My diet plan was becoming bigger and bigger and harder and harder to cope with. It was explained to me that as I gained weight, my body would adjust to the diet it was consuming; changing the rate of my metabolism. Therefore, in order for me to keep gaining weight, my diet had to be increased on a regular basis: A large banana had been added to my cereal in the mornings; another two yogurts had been added-one to my lunch and one to my tea, (which now meant I was eating four a day), and it was said that I had to have a pudding from the menu at least once a week. I did not do puddings. My heart was pounding as I ran my eyes across the gruesome descriptions of the foods I had to eat. But I couldn't show it. Not when I had to make a good impression of myself. I thought that, yes-okay, I might put some weight on whilst I'm waiting for the tribunal hearing to take place, but when they let me out, (which I truly believed they would), I would eat minimal to ensure the fastest weight loss. Besides, it was better than having to complete the whole process without the tribunal hearing, and gain the total amount of weight Dr.Waissel was pushing me for. But I couldn't believe it, apparently there was a long waiting list for patients to have tribunal meetings: eight weeks to be exact. That meant eight weeks of solid weight gain. It was time to put my plan into action.

Monday morning came and I woke at 4am to wash my hair. I rushed like mad so I had time to prepare for what I called, 'operation suckers'! I locked myself in the bathroom at eight o'clock with the cup I used for washing my paintbrushes in, and filled it to the brim. I necked the water and refilled and refilled the glass; downing each one until I felt completely sick. I drank until my tummy was bloated and sore, but this still wouldn't be enough. I'd brought four heavy rocks which I'd painted on a holiday in Devon that reminded me of the happy times we'd spent together as a family. Instead of looking at them though, I stuffed one of them into my knickers, along with four batteries tied together with a bobble for extra weight.

My pyjama pants were baggy and disguised the lumpy bulges quite well. This was the perfect plan. Each time I'd get weighed, I'd simply increase the amount I drank, and place a heavier weight in my pants! Brilliant, genius! Although, when it came to walking down the corridor to the treatment room, I was bricking it, as I was nervous that the weights would fall to the floor; ruining my plans and revealing my true inner feelings about the weight I was gaining. But it was a risk I had to take. It was better than not trying at all. This trick would hopefully delay diet increases too, for if they saw my weight increasing at such a rate, there wouldn't be a need to increase my calorie intake and so my 'real' weight wouldn't increase as quickly.

   I received a phone call the following afternoon. It was concerning Barry. He was in a bad way and had been rushed to Christie's hospital the night before in a turn for the worse. My heart sank and just added to my list of worries. I was pleased, however, for the fact that Dr.Waissel had been so generous as to let me out for two hours that evening with my parents to visit him in hospital. I hadn't realised how seriously ill he was until we turned a corner into his hospital room: he was strapped to a bed; an oxygen mask covering his drained, white face which was usually jolly and pink. He was ever so pleased to see us, but couldn't manage to talk much as it was too much energy for him to find. I told him that I'd been working on a painting for him, (as he'd always secretly wanted one from me), and that I'd never stop painting. He was so limp and weak that we had to lift a drink to his mouth for him to be able to suck the brown liquid through the straw. Even though he was in such a critical state, his only concern was for my health and just wanted to know I'd be okay. This put my problems into perspective: I had it easy; at least I wasn't lying on my death bed counting my last moments before I'd exit the world forever. For a moment, I even told myself to 'buck my ideas up' and to eat like a normal person, as one should treasure the privilege of a healthy body and preserve that for as long as it is possible. I gave him a huge squeeze at the end of our visit and took a prolonged look at him, incase it was the last memory I'd have of one of the biggest inspirational characters in my life. I loved him and it wasn't fair that this was happening to him and he was only in his fifties.

Back at the ward that night, I was highly emotional, and I did not want to eat a thing. But part of me said that Barry wouldn't have wanted him to prevent me from eating and getting better, so, for Barry, I ate my supper in a difficult silence.

This is where the group, 'Art therapy' came in handy. It was my favourite group as I loved art and you could be as creative as you liked. We had tasks of expressing our emotions through the visual language of art. I remember one piece I produced which represented anger and frustration. I made this by throwing and splattering red and black paint on paper and overlapping this with aggressive words made up of letters cut from magazines and newspapers. I then tore away at the edges to resemble how pointless I thought being in hospital was.

A few days later, Barry had passed away. I wept down the phone to my mum, who was also in tears.

"I wish I was there with you Amy. I should be there for you; I'm your mum, and this hospital business is preventing me from being with you." I wanted to throw my arms around her and sob into her soft, blonde hair that always smelt familiarly of hairspray and perfume. This was the first encounter of death I'd ever had to cope with, and I didn't take it well.

For the next few days, my food proved too much for me; never mind how much I wanted to prove myself, I just couldn't bring myself to eat it. The nurses decided to separate me from the others and thought that 1:1 support was needed at meal times, as I was crying and refusing food in front of the other young people at every meal.

It was so nerve racking sitting at a small round table by myself opposite a nursing staff whilst trying to eat. I felt like a goldfish: the outsiders staring in whilst I sat there uncomfortably; not knowing where to look. The silence was irritating. The only sound I could hear was made by my own chewing, and this reminded me even more of eating. But with this tedious process came benefits. One evening after the chef had brought the tea up to the ward, my plate sat alone in the isolated room waiting for a nurse to take me in to eat it. The staff were running late on meal preparations that particular evening, and so were tied-up in a manic hurry in the kitchen. I checked the coast was clear and darted into the little room where my plate sat sweating under a cling film roof. With trembling hands, in fright of being caught, I pulled at one side of the cling film and grabbed a big piece of lamb dripping in gravy from the plate. I noticed the window was open which backed onto the adult garden a story below, so I chucked it flying out the window to the ground. I quickly wrapped the cling film back under the plate and hoped I wasn't in eye sight when I ran at top speed out the room and into my bedroom, closing the door behind me. My cheeks felt flushed and the sense of adrenaline was overwhelming. I couldn't help but giggle to myself- the thought of an adult patient lay innocently on a deckchair below, when all of a sudden this sopping wet slab of meat comes soaring through the air and onto their face! The suckers. Honestly. It was *that* easy!

    That night, I shared the details of my victory amongst the other girls. They were squealing with laughter and couldn't believe I actually had the nerve to attempt such a risky action; especially when I was trying to prove myself! They kept trying to wind me up by hinting at what I'd done every time a member of staff loitered around, but I was quick to shove a sock in it. That was the first night I'd felt part of 'the gang'. All the previous nights I'd spent cooped up in my room, but now I was in on the sneaky discussions; planning little stunts together and our friendships grew.

    The phone rang the next morning, early. It was my dad. I wondered what he wanted as it was usually my mum that phoned, and rarely before lunch. His voice sounded like he had something good to say and was quick to break the news to me: Barry's will had been read, and it turned out that he had left all of his art equipment, right down to the art desks and the lamps, to me. I was speechless. Tears did the talking. A real warm, happy feeling glowed inside me and I just couldn't believe it. Out of the hundreds of students, adults and children of all ages which he'd taught ever since before I was born, he chose to leave it all to me: Amy Lewis- a small and weird little college student. From that moment I realised how close Barry and I really were and recognised the potential he saw in me. This was it now. I was going to dedicate my life to my dream of becoming the next best thing since Walt Disney! We'd always talked about it and ironically came up with the name, 'Lewis Land'- a magical place where all *my* dreams became a reality and *my* characters pranced around in parades! Accept it didn't quite have the same ring to it as 'Disney Land'. Never again would I need any more art materials to full fill my artistic 'bursts': Artist's watercolours, quality watercolour paper, gouache, acrylics, oils, masses of the finest brushes, plates, sponges; everything I could possibly need. I wished he was there so I could tell him how much I appreciated his generosity. Dr.Waissel had been really mean and hadn't let me attend his funeral as I hadn't made enough 'progress' apparently. I didn't even have the chance to say goodbye.

   Recreation was a trip to Crosby beach. I was mega excited, even though it was an incredibly dull and windy day which would totally destroy my hair. It was my first proper time off the ward since admission, and it was a chance for a bit of exercise! However, I wasn't allowed to walk very far. But how could you go to a beach and not walk a fair distance? Me, Nikita, (a day patient who spent a couple of days a week with us), and Lizzie were allowed to go this week and Amanda and Michael, two rather amusing nursing assistants, took us there in the hospital mini van. The only down side to the trip was the long drive there and back. It's not that we were bored; it was the amount of calories we were preserving by sitting all that time.
   When we got there we weren't allowed to go anywhere until we ate our snacks. I didn't want anything but was desperate to get up and walk to burn some of the food off. Nikita and Lizzie were quick to hurry ahead whilst I tagged behind, half walking, half running, wanting to catch up but being weary to stick to the rules- not to 'walk too fast'!
   "Get walking you lazy slob. You've done nothing but eat all day."
   I ran to catch up with the others, but Amanda was quick to stop me, "You know you're not supposed to be walking, never

mind running. Slow down or we'll go back to the ward." I rolled my eyes and slowed down until she and Michael caught up with me. The walkway that lead onto the beach was piled high at both sides with mounds of dry sand, so I walked on them instead because it took extra effort to drag your feet through. By this time the wind was so strong that I looked like I'd been dragged through a hedge backwards- twice! This made me feel tense and I could hear the mirror calling me at the back of my mind. But no matter how breezy it was outside, I did not want to go back to that ward, so I kept on walking, trying to forget about how I looked. A group of good looking teenage boys, about the same age as me, were walking in our direction, (oh what bad timing that was)! I wanted to smile at them, as some part of me wanted to be liked by a boy, but I looked terrible. I'd never had a boyfriend before- only stupid boys at school taking- the-mick out of how 'swotty' I was; so I was longing for one. Lizzie and Nikita smiled at them but I looked the other way to the soggy shore and felt really cut-off from everyone else.

After a stroll, (or a crawl I'd describe it as), we had to turn back, but bantered to walk along the wet sand in search for shells. We found loads: curly ones, stripy ones, ones with little animals still living inside; all sorts! They were crammed, full of moist sand, into our pockets until we had to use our hands as pockets as well. When I stared out at the faraway sea, human figures made from rusted iron loomed, dotted here and there all over the beach. I'd heard about these: Antony Gormley was the artist responsible. They weren't particularly my ideal image of 'art'. They were a bit bland to me. But they immediately reminded me of my college art teacher, Ms.Elliott, who had a very broad knowledge of all kinds of art.

I'd received a brown envelope addressed to me a couple of days before, with handwriting on the front that I recognised: it was from Ms.Elliott.

She was coming to visit me and I was so excited to see her, but nervous at the same time incase she noticed any extra weight on me since the last time we'd seen each other. There were two other letters in there as well. One from Ms.Emary, the seemingly 'scary', yet extremely sarcastic textiles teacher, who told me a rather humorous little anecdote about her trip to see River dance,

Hi Amy

See what you think to these possible links. Please don't worry if you don't like them.

We thought that there might be a halfway point between the doll and a jack in a box, in that they introduce the idea of a box or container/jar.

Hope you are settling in ok. We all miss you. Planning to visit after Easter but will contact you so I can fit in with your other visitors.

love Lina

Dear Amy

Just thought I would write a note to say I am thinking of you and hope that you are not feeling too poorly. Think though of all the drawing you will be able to do – I do hope that they will allow you to do some work.

Last night I went with Mrs White (a biology teacher) to see Riverdance in Manchester. I have to say it really was most odd. Have you seen it? I know its been around for a long time and been on the tele as well, I hadn't seen it before. Anyway, all it is, is a lot of Irish dancing with no story, so of course they have to concoct something otherwise it wouldn't flow, so they came up with the idea of the Irish people leaving Ireland to settle in other countries where there is also a strong tradition of dancing. eg. America, Spain Russia etc. All most bizarre, as they were trying to mix all these different types of dance. However, I did enjoy the dancing. Not so sure about the singing though and the graphics on set, were appalling.

So now I want to go and learn Irish dancing! Can you imagine, well no perhaps not.

I am hoping to get some exercise by joining Kate's (our technician's) rounders team. I have become a bit of a slob recently, although still go to tai chi every week.

> We are all very busy here marking Personal Studies (U6 projects) and also the U6 exams have just started - so everything is a little hectic.
> However it will all get done eventually.
> Anyway Amy, I'm sure you've read enough of all this drivel. Hope you are managing to keep busy.
> Take care
> Lots of love
> Julie Emary
> XXX

and one from my graphics teacher, Katherine, who was leaving soon so I probably wasn't going to see her again and she wanted to wish me all the best.

> Hello Amy,
>
> hope you are doing ok and I just wanted to let you know that you're missed. The work that you produce is beautiful and you are very talented. I will hopefully see you soon, keep your spirits up!!
> love from
> Kathryn.

. Finally, at the bottom of the envelope was an A4 piece of paper with get well wishes written all over it from my class mates in art, which I stuck on the front of the bathroom door in my room.

These letters and little messages meant so much to me. I

40

read them over and over and felt touched by how many people took some time to think about me. Letters played a big part in the build-up to my discharge, as they reminded me of the people who care about me, and of the outside world which I was missing.

On the way back to the ward, I texted Ms.Elliott to tell her about my trip to Crosby beach, and she was rather jealous because she was stuck in college marking all day… tee hee! But to tell you the truth, I would have much preferred to be trapped in college marking than being in the care of people who had the right to force-feed me.

The next trip I had to look forward to was an hour's drive with my parents. I couldn't tell you the time that passed between these visits, as the only time that seemed real was when I spent it with my family and friends from home. All other time seemed to wither away into what felt like a never ending spiral of conflict between me and anorexia.

"Oh my god, I'm actually sitting in our car!" It felt so weird to be that excited about this, since I'd always taken car rides for granted and ever since I'd been staying at hospital, I was beginning to think I'd never step foot into our car again. I was only allowed to either stay seated in the car or visit a park or somewhere where we could sit on a bench. It was a bright day so we went to the garden centre just round the corner. I thought, 'stuff the not walking! I'm with my family doing a normal family activity, so if I want to have a stroll around, I will!' We did have a brief mooch around at the gifts and novelties, but my parents soon felt the need to retreat to the café for me to sit down. Regardless of the limited time I had with my family, it significantly improved my mood, which was noted by all staff members. Although after a while, the fears of eating kicked in again.

"*This little vendetta won't carry on much longer you know. Okay, you're going out with your family where people can notice how much thinner you are than others around you, but that ain't gonna be for much longer. You're going to get fat, and then you're not going to want to go out anymore. Why let everybody witness the new curves that have grown on your thighs? I'd hide myself away if I was you. What is the point of living anymore?"*

    I'd noticed that if I appeared to look happy, the nurses watched me less carefully; giving me more opportunities to persuade them for the much wanted home leave that I desperately wanted, (in order to see my family and to prevent further weight gain). Even though I forced the corners of my mouth upwards into a teeth-grinding smile, my internal emotions were telling another story and as the next weigh-in came, I realised my devious little plan was going to become much harder to carry out. I'd downed my tenth glass of water and just couldn't drink any more. I was absolutely bursting for the toilet and there was twenty minutes to go before I got weighed. I walked round in fast circles to distract myself from the urge, but the pain was too much and I rushed to the toilet. This was so frustrating, if I couldn't handle the consumption of such a volume then, how on earth was I supposed to be able to handle it in a few weeks time? I had to resort to plan B. Instead of one rock and a bundle of batteries, I placed an extra rock in my knickers, inside another pair of knickers and practiced walking in a convincing fashion inside my locked bathroom. The nurse, soon after, called me in to get weighed. I'd gained again, obviously, due to the rocks. But how was I supposed to know if I had actually put any real weight on or not? I didn't know the weights of those rocks. What if I was getting fatter but was unaware of it? This would be terrible as I'd be totally oblivious to it and therefore feel even less in control. I also hated the fact that the nurses had to read a weight that was more than my proper mass, as I felt ashamed to be seen as that measurement. I also didn't want them to change their views about me.

    Breakfast came next and I really struggled. I sat there and stared at the cup of apple juice and felt my already bloated stomach. As not to make it too obvious that I'd in fact already drank gallons that morning, I sipped a little of it and slowly picked at my cereal. I ended up passing my drink onto snack, where I still couldn't force myself to drink, so at lunch I ended up with three lots of drink and I just sucked them all up as quickly as I could through a straw and retreated to my bed to lie down. When was this going to end?

The next day was mother's day, and my mum was coming with my dad and my brother and sister for the first time to see me. Before we had our visits some of us were allowed to go on a walk to pick some daffodils as a mother's day present. But I wasn't. Even though I'd put weight on, I hadn't gained enough. How much bloody weight did they want me to gain? I knew what was coming next too: another diet increase. I asked Sharon to pick some flowers for me to give to my mum instead, and she came back with a lovely big bunch which I tied together with some pretty ribbon. My mum loved them, and my homemade card I'd spent ages on the night before. She was worth every last delicate petal and more. My mum was priceless! I was pleased to see my brother and sister too, as I'd not seen them in a while and surprisingly missed the arguing!

That visit went really well and I was looking forward to seeing them again soon. However, my mood changed when Moira took me into my room and asked me what I'd like increasing on my diet. 'Err, hmmm; let me think about that one...what do you think?!' She was being serious though. I had had another increase and they needed to ask me where I thought I could manage more food. This was ridiculous; they were having a bloody giggle. I couldn't think of anything else to do but cry. My chest hurt I cried so much, but that wasn't going to stop the increase. After a number of conflicts I eventually said that they could put a couple of rich tea biscuits in at snacks if they really had to. As soon as she left, I was having none of it and immediately began planning ways in which to secrete the food back to my room where it could be disposed of down the toilet. I'm quite pleased about my choice of increase because biscuits, (especially light rich teas), were the easiest thing to dispose of.

The next morning, having slept on the situation, I felt more confident with my plans to secrete food back to my room. But that pleasurable feeling didn't last long. I heard a faint wrap at my door. I opened it slightly and there stood Fay, holding up a pale blue gown in front of her.

"Morning Amy, we need to do a spot weigh so please could you take off your pajamas and knickers and put the gown on?" Shit! The rocks... they were in my draw, and I had no time to down mug after mug of water. I thought quickly and came to the solution that I'd slip the rocks into my knickers when I was changing.

"Erm, yeah, okay. I'll be one minute." I replied and began to close the door. Fay's foot came out and kept it open.

"No, I need to stay with you whilst you change." My heart dropped; I could've fainted. They were going to find out my secret. What was I going to do? As I turned around, I rolled my eyes and gritted my teeth. My face was in an expression of panic, and I slowly started to blush. She lead me down the corridor; the other patients staring and whispering in the lounge behind me, and my heart beat rang through my ears. I followed her into a room and my bare feet made contact with the icy cold floor. A chill ran through my bones as I stepped on the scales. I closed my eyes shut, scrunched my nose and tensed my shoulders so they were touching the bottom of my ear lobes. I looked like I was nervously awaiting a blood test to be over and done with. Silence. Fay said nothing, but her eyes said it all. They peered over the edge of her spectacles which were balanced on the tip of her pointy nose and she scribbled something onto her clipboard. Once I'd returned to my room I shut the door and heaved a sigh of defeat.

"Bloody hell!" I got dressed and then another, louder knock sounded on my door. Fay re-entered, closing it behind her. She towered above me, sheltering me with her long shadow.

"Now, Amy," she began, peeping over her glasses which were perched on the end of her nose, "Would you happen to know why today you are two kilograms lighter than a couple of days ago?" I thought for a moment, still glancing up at her.

"Erm, really?" I asked. "Not a clue, sorry. They must be broken!" I offered her a cheeky, yet innocent grin, raising both my eyebrows, and she returned a suspicious glare; then exited. Biting my bottom lip I resumed getting dressed.

Now that I was in a really bad mood, things didn't get any easier and Kelly was kidding around with me by pretending to 'have it in' for me. I was in no mood for jokes, so decided to cause some trouble, just to lighten things up a little! At lunch, I had observed that on a number of occasions Kelly had taken her own bottle of orange squash to the table. I used this knowledge to my advantage and made sure I was sat next to her. During supervision, she got up from the table and sauntered to the window. I took this opportunity to quickly swipe the bottle, pour in a small sachet of salt I'd nicked from the ward kitchen earlier, and put the bottle back in its original position. Ellie exchanged a cheeky grin across the table and gave me a thumbs up. My heart was pounding. I'd never have thought I'd be capable of doing something so evil! But that was how frustrated I was about being there. During supervision I eyed the bottle whenever Kelly approached it, but she never took a sip. Afterwards, during Kelly's break, we all joked about the prank together outside the lounge area and imagined her face scrunch up into a wince once she'd tasted it. A few jokes later however, Kelly came back to the ward with a face like thunder. And I knew.

"YOU. ROOM. NOW!" She said sternly, directed at me. "I'll be in in a minute." I walked to my room unable to shift the smile that had appeared on my face. I couldn't believe she'd sent me to my room. I mean, it wasn't even *my* room; she wasn't my mum! I sat on my bed with a heart beat of a race horse. How did she know it was me though? Had she seen me? Had someone said something? I was in two minds of what to do. I was either going to have to lie and say I didn't have any idea what she was talking about, or I was going to have to admit it and face up to the consequences. The door opened and she came in, closing it behind her. My smile disappeared. She stood with folded arms in silence and gave me a shameful look.

"Putting salt into someone's drink!" She said in a low voice, unimpressed.
"You wouldn't like it if I put salt in your drinks when I prepare them for you." I actually felt really bad, but at least this took my mind off what was really happening to me.

"I'm sorry Kelly, I'm finding things really difficult at the moment; I wasn't thinking." I tried, but her facial expression didn't budge.

"No one wants to be here any less than you do, but that doesn't give you the right to act inappropriately."

"Sorry. I'm really sorry. I didn't mean it."

"Stay in your room and think about what you've done. Don't come out until you have." She left. My heart was beating one million times a minute! The adrenaline felt great; I'd achieved something. I couldn't wipe the mischievous grin off my face, although part of me felt bad. It wasn't like me at all to do something like that, but anorexia was controlling every aspect of me: my mind, my actions, my potential future- it has the power to change a person.

Later that night Ms.Elliott was coming to visit me. I was dead excited, but hovered round my bedroom door fidgeting; anxious at what she might think of me. Michael told me not to be nervous because she would be looking forward to seeing me, not coming to judge me. I knew this but it would be my first real interaction with the outside world since I started to gain weight. It was hard enough to cope with the weight gain in an enclosed unit which was cut off from everything else, but being able to cope with it whilst around other people was another matter. I had a little time to calm myself down though because she'd sent me a text to say she'd got lost and so would be a little late! Eventually, there was a buzz at the door. Ms.Elliott came in and threw her arms around me and I was so pleased to see her. I briefly showed her round my bedroom but was ushered to the visiting room as I wasn't allowed to stand up for too long. The visit went great. We chatted about my course work I was doing for art and showed her my sketch books I'd been working on. Concentrating on college made me feel a part of the college again, and for a moment I forgot I was even in hospital. I told her about the gross size of my diet… and, may have mentioned one or two of my shenanigans! We laughed, but she reminded me that I was there to gain the weight to become healthy again and I knew that, but I was ready to try everything and anything to prevent that from happening. To keep my spirits high I told her about the advocate I'd contacted to support me in my tribunal case. This was the only sense of hope I had to hold onto, and I was determined to win that case. However, Ms.Elliott's reaction told me that it wasn't going to work and that I needed to be in there, but I wasn't going to accept that. It was reassuring that she said I didn't look any different than last time we saw each other. I didn't know what I was worrying about. It hadn't seemed ten minutes when Diane, (a night staff), came in and told me it was snack in five minutes. My heart sank. I didn't want Ms.Elliott to go. I wanted her to take me home with her; away from the hospital, and I didn't want more food. Before she left, she handed me a gift bag with some presents in it. Awww, she didn't have to; I was so touched. I really appreciated this lovely thought and I felt really good inside. She gave me one last big hug and told me she'd come and visit again. I couldn't wait for that. I was so lucky to have people that cared so much about me. I resentfully said good bye and she left the ward.

After snack, I kneeled next to my bed and peered inside the gift bag. I pulled out a lovely pink note/sketch book made with really old handmade paper, a little box of cute animal magnetic toys, a packet of magnetic page clips in the shape of cartoon cats and a large tube of white acrylic paint which I really needed. These were great; really me. I'd made it known at college that I loved pink and anything small and cute and these were just perfect!

As the nights slowly passed, they became more and more unbearable. I'd lie on my back, uncomfortable on the breathing air bed, feeling where my protruding bones were disappearing. Instead, more skin seemed to cover these areas. I did not like it. I didn't like it one bit. The scariest part was not knowing how much weight they would make me gain. They wouldn't give me a target weight, as they told me that each individual was different and it depended on what I looked like at the end of my treatment. What sort of an excuse was that? 'Oh, sorry love, you're not fat enough yet, let's see how you look in a couple of stones time!' Err, I don't think so! I couldn't stand this anymore. I needed to get out of there. I had dreams about escape routes I could take, but there was always a flaw in my plan: either there were too many nurses on duty or guilt took over me so I couldn't face it.

'SMASH!' Everyone rushed to the dining room. Fay had moved the glass dining table and it had shattered into hundreds of jagged pieces. This was absolutely great, and brilliant timing too! This meant that for health and safety reasons, we weren't allowed to get another glass table: No more being able to see what went on under there. It was replaced with a wooden one- much easier to smuggle food away out of sight under! My new diet plan had started and biscuits were strictly not allowed to pass my lips. That was a rule; far too calorific. But with this new non-see-through privilege came opportunities, which were much too rare to ignore. I figured that if I broke the biscuits up into pieces then crumbs would fall out; saving me from a few calories. These pieces could then be discretely slotted into my boots one by one. Obviously I'd have to put a few pieces in my mouth so they could see I was eating them, but that didn't mean I had to swallow them did it? All I had to do was store them there for half an hour through supervision and then empty them down the toilet- simple! I soon realised this technique would come in handy for hiding bits of sandwich too.

My supervised meal on the ward with my parents came and I really didn't see the point of it. I was used to eating with my parents. Just because some other patients wouldn't eat in front of their family didn't mean that I couldn't. It was really frustrating that I had to go through this unnecessary process before I was allowed to have day leave. Anyway, we sat in the community room around a small wooden table being monitored by a member of staff. I really was not in the mood to eat that day, but I had to, otherwise the nurses would think I couldn't eat with my parents and then I'd never be allowed home. So, I sat there with a brave face resentfully forcing the sandwiches, yogurt and fruit down my throat. Once I'd finished I felt like saying, 'see, do you believe me now? I'm not anorexic just because I prefer to eat healthy food. You've just witnessed me eat without a problem in the company of my family, so I think I deserve to go home now, don't you?' I was really pleased with myself. Not for the fact I'd eaten, but because I'd proven them wrong; they didn't know me as well as they thought they did.

And so it was confirmed that the following weekend I could go home after breakfast and return after tea. This was the best news I'd had so far, and was the biggest opportunity I'd had to miss foods out.

Chester zoo: that was the next trip for recreation to aim for. Ellie hadn't been on recreation for a long, long while and I could tell she really wanted to go this time; not to see the animals of course, but to go hiking around the huge zoo! She was only allowed to go if she drank everything orally for twenty four hours. She was on drinks and had recently, after months of being on the tube, had it removed. I was so proud of her, but I knew how difficult she found things. Tears would stream down her face when the staff put the straw to her mouth and she would shake her legs.

"Come on Ellie", I tried at meal times, "you can drink it. The walk will be worth it, and besides, what's worse: having to drink the drink but being able to work some of it off, or having it forced down a tube anyway and not being able to leave the ward to exercise?" I could tell she knew the best answer and I knew she wanted to drink it to get out of there, but it was so hard for her. Eventually though, after a whole day of persuading, she'd done it.

"Well done mate, you've done great."

Whilst Ellie had made her first step forward, another patient on the ward was having the worst time of her life. Screams and shouts filled the ward's corridors and muffled sounds of struggling echoed. It was Emily: a quiet, pretty girl whose personality seemed to have been absorbed by anorexia. She didn't talk much and when she did it was as quiet as a whisper. I felt really sorry for her, as I knew how difficult having to put weight on was and I felt like screaming most of the time too. I wanted to get to know her and become friends, but I didn't know how to approach her. Soon the news broke out that she had been put on bed rest, which meant she was not allowed out of her room at all and had a 1:1 staff member with her all hours of the day and night. I'd noticed things were getting too tough for her to handle because during every supervision after her drinks of Fortijuice, she'd sit with her head in her hands, (one hand being over her mouth), and I knew she wasn't swallowing the last few mouthfuls. But where was she getting rid of the drink? She was on bathroom lock-up so it couldn't have been down the drain. Bed rest meant she couldn't get away with this anymore which made matters even tougher.

Lizzie was eligible to come on recreation as well as Ellie and me. We'd have a great time! When the day of recreation came, Carmina and a member of staff from downstairs, called Sal, were chosen to take us. My biggest worry though was that it was lunch time when we arrived and if Ellie didn't drink her Fortijuice we'd have to turn straight back. The situation was made even more daunting as we were eating in a public area, which really frightened her. Her brows furrowed and crinkled her face in anxiety, but we were there to support her. Meanwhile, I had some stinky tuna sandwiches that I managed to break up and hide three quarters of in my coat pockets under the wooden bench. And after a toilet break, (and the bon-voyage to some smelly, fishy bread), we were finally aloud to make a start round the zoo. We were quick to rush off but were told to slow down.

The baby elephants were so cute; they were pushing each other down the muddy banking and squirting water like garden sprinklers and their trumpeting was fantastically loud. Five minutes into the trip, my mobile rang. It was Barbara the advocate I'd contacted. What a perfect place to ring me up!

"Hello? Hello?" She began.

"Oh, hello Barbara", I addressed in my best voice, "I am terribly sorry for the disturbance from the other patients!" (Referring to the noisy elephants in the background); Ellie gave me a shove. "Not really, we're at a zoo on a day trip", I explained. She'd rang to organise a date for the following week where she could come and meet with me on the ward to discuss my situation. I scribbled the information she gave me on my hand and felt content that another step had been made in my release from that nightmare. It was a privilege to have our phones. My dad had bought me a really cheap £9.99 one from Tesco, as camera phones were not allowed on the ward, understandably, as pictures could have been taken for comparison purposes between patients.

We were really enjoying the trip, but I couldn't help but feel emotional as I had always been there with my family and never had I once considered I'd be there as part of a hospital group. It brought back precious memories from previous visits and I longed to have my family there with me instead of strangers who I hardly knew. The monkey houses were bursting with lively little whippets swinging from the roofs and chasing one another. How I longed to be a monkey at that moment: free, happy; without a care in the world. They must have it easy. All they live off is fruit, which would've been ideal for me. The bat cave was really daunting for Carmina. She took one peep inside the murky cave and retreated a good distance away. Me, Ellie and Lizzie however were itching to have some alone time without being monitored like youths in a detention centre, so there was no stopping us from entering! I felt safe in that really dark, hollow crevice in the stone wall. No one could see what I looked like and I couldn't see anyone else to compare myself to. It was as though the rich darkness had engulfed all of my worries. Bats swooped over our heads from all directions and Ellie shrieked, "Aaah!"

"Please don't scream", a zoo keeper demanded, "you'll frighten the bats!" Ellie giggled and we hurried back to the entrance in the wall.

Once we'd seen the whole zoo, it started to pour it down. Sudden panic thudded to my chest: my hair. What was I going to do? We'd only one umbrella between us. I looked around and everyone else seemed quite relaxed about the heavy drops of water spilling from the sky. 'Why couldn't I be like that?' And so for the first time, I thought, 'Sod it. It's not a life or death situation. Come on Amy; act normal for once in your life.' I stood still watching Carmina, Sal, Lizzie and Ellie fade into the crowds and I tipped my head back as far as it could go. The rain trickled over my eyelids and stuck my fringe to my face and I felt my troubles being washed away with the rain. I ran to catch up with the others, blending in with everyone around me and actually enjoying getting soaked. Even if that did mean I looked like I'd just taken a bath. The last stop was the gift shop. I'd brought some of the money my relatives had given me to spend and decided to get something for Emily, since she wasn't allowed to come. I'd noticed she had an interest in reading and spotted a black leather bookmark with shiny rainbow engravings of the zoo on the front. It was perfect. I also bought a few gifts for my family and something for Brooke, as her eighth birthday was coming up.

    My bubble was burst when I returned to the ward. I'd forgotten about my CPA. This was a meeting for Dr.Waissel, me and my parents and everyone else involved with my care. It was to discuss my progress and to decide on future action. I saw my Cahms worker enter the ward and my heart sank. It was him that had been trying to force me into a hospital for weeks before I was admitted. It was him that did all the over exaggerating. He used to look at me like I had six heads; as though I was about to drop dead.

    "Get your coat on", he used to demand, "You look frozen." But I wasn't. He'd take my blood pressure with anxiety pasted on his face; eyes squinted inwards and the corners of his mouth squeezed into tight knots. 'What a palaver' I thought. Dr.Waissel hurried down the corridor and lead about eight people into the community room, two of which were my parents. I had the choice to go into the meeting or not. This was a stupid choice to make: of course I was going to bloody go in! I wanted to know exactly what they were saying about me and this was a perfect opportunity to plea for discharge. I wasn't just going to let some strangers take total control over my life without my input. But I had to have snack first. I don't think I had ever eaten snack so fast, but I couldn't hide anything incase something fell out and rolled into the middle of the carpet in my CPA. Feeling rather sick and guilty I went into the meeting. Chairs were arranged in a circular fashion around the room, coffee tables piled high with plates of biscuits and mugs of brown tea in the centre. I took a seat next to my mum and held her hand tight. The stuffy room fell silent and all eyes were on me.

    "Welcome to the first of Amy's CPAs", Dr.Waissel announced. "I'm Dr.Waissel, in charge of the eating disorders unit." We went round the room introducing ourselves; there was the dietician, Kathy the therapist, my Cahms worker, Carmina, my mum and dad, me, Li the school teacher and a couple of others. When Dr.Waissel had said, 'welcome to the *first* of Amy's CPAs", I felt sick: how many of these was I going to have? They were every four to six weeks so no one was planning to discharge me any time soon. We all had sheets noted with the history of my health, the reason for my admission, a copy of my current diet plan and statements written by certain nurses; one being from me, in which I made it specifically clear that I hated being there and I wanted to go home. But from all this information, the numbers in bold at the top of the page were the hardest for me to read. They were my admission weight and my current weight. So now not only did I myself know for a fact that I'd gained weight, everyone else did too and it was there in black and white to haunt me forever. There was no escaping this reality.

"Look at that. Just look at what you've allowed to happen to you. Call yourself an anorexic? You're pathetic!"

Basically, each member of the meeting said they all agreed that I was in the best place and that I wasn't ready to leave yet as I was still at a very dangerous weight. They shared with everyone how my mind wasn't psychologically coping with the weight gain. They were talking as if I wasn't even there. I shook my head all the way through and tears swelled in my eyes, but I concealed them as I didn't want to make it obvious I was struggling. When it came to my dad's turn to say how he felt I was really angry towards him. He said he was pleased I was gaining weight and that he thought I was in the best place and shouldn't come out until I'm ready. What did he know anyway? I was me and only I knew what was best for me. I wouldn't look at him and clutched my mum's hand tighter. When it came to her turn I could tell she wasn't comfortable in that situation; I'd been pleading her every night to tell the nurses to let me out and to say that she knew how I felt and knew what was best for me, so I felt as though I was pressuring her.

"Erm, I think Amy is doing well with the treatment... She obviously doesn't want to be here and would appreciate discharge as soon as it is possible." I knew she had other feelings to express, but didn't. After the meeting I was allowed ten minutes alone with my parents before tea and I really let my dad know how I felt about him.

"You like it that I'm locked up in here don't you?" I screamed through gritted teeth. "You'll only be happy when I'm all curvy and podgy. Mum knows how I feel and she cares about me. I hate you." There was an awkward silence. I really wished I hadn't said that; of course I didn't hate him, I was only angry at the difficult situation I was in and let it all out on my dad as though he was a human punch bag. After a really horrible ten minutes, my mum and dad left for tea.

That evening, I sauntered up to Emily's room holding the leather bookmark I'd gotten her. I peered round the door and she was lay awake on her bed; a nurse sat in a chair at the other end. She beamed a smile when she saw me and sat up. I handed her the bookmark and her eyes lit up; it really meant a lot to her that she was being thought of and I wished she could have come out into the lounge to join us.

"Thank you", she said in a soft whispery voice. I gave her a hug and retreated to the lounge feeling pleased I'd made another friend.

Me, Ellie, Sharon, Amber and Lizzie sunk ourselves into black squishy bean bags in the lounge and gathered round 'the pamper box', which we'd ask to be unlocked from the cupboard. Lizzie popped 'Sister Act' into the video player and we whispered secretly amongst ourselves whilst painting our nails sparkly pink and listening to the joyful singing nuns in the background.

"I can't stand it here anymore", I shared, "How do you cope with it?"

"We don't cope, we just pretend to," Replied Ellie. "But I tell you what; as soon as I'm out of here I'm losing all the weight again."

"Me too", I added. Lizzie was sat awkwardly on the sofa opposite and I could tell she didn't want to discuss weight, so I tried to change the subject.

"What are you doing tonight Lizzie?" I asked. She shrugged.

"Dunno. Probably speak to my mum on the phone then get a bath."

"Aw, that's nice." I tried, but not much later Sharon was quick to direct our thoughts back onto the subject of weight.

"So, how much do you weigh then?" She asked me, "You in your twenties?" (By this she meant 20 -29 kg.)

"Thirties", I reluctantly replied. Her eyes widened.

"God, you don't look that!" I felt dead good. Other people obviously saw me as thin, which really boosted my confidence. However, other patients must have been in their twenties when admitted, otherwise she wouldn't have asked. A feeling of unworthiness drifted over me, and my mind began trying to picture someone so thin. I envied those images.

After snack we all, except from Lizzie who'd taken a bath, retreated back to the lounge. I was dying to ask if anyone had ever attempted an escape, but I didn't want to hint that I was considering it myself. The urge proved too much though, and I asked Ellie.

"Have you ever tried to escape?"

"Yeah", she replied. Relief! I wasn't the only one who felt like I did. "Didn't last long though. I was stood over there", she explained, pointing to a spot at the opposite side of the room, "and I said, 'Right, I'm escaping', so I legged it out of the ward."

"Then what happened?" I asked with intense curiosity.

"I collapsed half way down the drive and Amanda, who'd been running after me, took me back to the ward." Wow! What an act of bravery. 'Although, maybe it wasn't such a wise thing to tell them you were escaping!' I thought. "Yup, then I got put on a 1:1 for a couple of weeks." Oh. Maybe it wasn't worth the risk then. Besides, the planning would have to be immaculate, and that's very hard to do when you're surrounded by spying nurses all day long that check on you every ten minutes. However, that night I did pick up on some useful advice that I'd hang onto for the rest of my admission: "Just play the game and you'll win." This was gold; absolute genius. If we let-on that we were complying with the program until we were discharged, it would come quicker and so sooner the opportunity to lose weight would come. I'd continuously repeat this to myself over and over to help me through the traumatic pain I felt whilst gaining weight, because at the back of my mind I knew I was the winner, (or so I thought).

The weekend finally came and I was so excited to be going home. I ate my breakfast quicker than usual so I could be gone sooner. I drifted off at the table and nurse Natasha had to shake me to wake me up. How embarrassing! I packed my vital items: my brush, bobbles and clips; hurried out of the ward and jumped into the car.

"Wow", my dad began, "Amy, you're coming home! This is great!" My dad and I were cheerful in each other's presence that morning. We'd forgotten about the other night.

As I opened the front door to our house the sweet smell of home seeped through my nostrils and I felt happy. My mum gave me an enormous hug and my brother and sister too. Everyone was pleased to see me. The house was sparkling, as always, but had an extra gleam as though my mum had done a special dust around just for me. My guinea pigs were still outside chunnering away in their high pitched squeaks. I could tell they recognised my voice. I'd missed them so much. On my desk upstairs I found a vase of beautiful red roses and two cards. It turned out that Daniel, (out of all people to spend his money), had bought the flowers for me specially. I can't actually say how much this meant to me. I really wanted to be close to my brother and I'd always thought he'd viewed me as some pathetic weirdo, but this made me feel closer to him. The other card was hand drawn by Brooke and really touched me that she'd missed me so much. I'd promised myself that I wouldn't spend my time on my hair once I was at home, as I wanted to make the most of the rare opportunity to spend time with my family. The daunting mirrors still loomed where I had left them and that taunting temptation to make myself look better slithered up my spine once more. I edged slowly towards them and knelt in front of the devils. As I stared into the reflection, conflicting thoughts, hatred, despise, 'the game', family, leaked into my mind. I looked fatter in my mirrors than at the hospital. I did my hair a couple of times until my mum shouted me. For once I found the strength to drag myself away from their clutches and went to my mum in the kitchen.

"Don't forget to have your snack", my mum reminded me. How could I forget? My mum had been to the supermarket specially to buy all the foods that I like. She bought watermelon, pineapple, strawberries, iced gems and all the best flavours of Muller light yogurt. I really did appreciate all their efforts so much and it just encouraged me to keep at 'the program' so I would be allowed home more and more and for longer periods.

I loved preparing my own snack- no scraping of the yogurt pot, a little less fruit juice and, watermelon, (the least calorific fruit of them all). I got up after snack but my mum told me to sit back down for supervision.

"Mum, I'm at home!" I reminded her.

"Yes I know, but we agreed that you'd comply with their rules whilst you are at home."

"But please. Come on, this isn't fair." I tried. I had fifteen minutes, which was better than half an hour, then my mum said it was alright to go. I spent most of the day downstairs loitering around my mum. I couldn't get enough of her presence and I felt angry that I had to go back to the hospital. It was good to eat tea at home; I loved my mum's cooking and, no offence to the cooks at the hospital but, she new how to cook a potato without it being as solid as a rock! I'd also noticed that the usual frequent arguing that took place everyday in our house between Daniel and Brooke was minimal. I knew my mum had secretly told them to behave for once as I was coming home; this made me feel really important, although, as much as I hated the arguing, I missed it too. I must have hugged and kissed her at least ten times and the last one before leaving was the hardest. We filled up with tears. "Don't cry," My mum comforted, "You'll be home again soon and hopefully for longer next time." I kept this thought in my mind and sadly slumped back into the car with my dad.

Back on the ward that night, I made it clear how much going home meant to me and how much happier I was after being in the presence of my parents. Hopefully I thought if I looked content enough, they may have considered letting me go home if I proved to be doing well away from the hospital. I strained a crescent- moon shaped smile to appear on my face; the corners turning upwards and my dimples deepening. However, my inner feelings were far from this; I was crying inside. Of course I was pleased to have been home with my family, but I was still a part of the hospital and wouldn't have been able to go home again until I'd gained even more weight. So what was the point? If I had to gain weight but become miserable in the process to be allowed home, I'd never enjoy being home with them again. The whole stupid thing was pointless and I was angry at everything and everyone.

Whilst I'd been home for the day, Lizzie had gone on her home leave: four whole days! *Four whole days* without nagging nurses, regular checks and plates after plates of food being thrust under your chins to finish. I wondered how she felt. Would I have that privilege one day? How long would I have to wait until it was my turn? Would it *ever* be my turn? Even though I was really pleased for her as she had been there a lot longer than I had, I couldn't help feeling envious of her position.

It felt different at supper. There was an empty space opposite me. I missed Lizzie. It had just occurred to me how we had all bonded since admission. The fact that we could all relate to each other and understand one another's feelings played a huge role in our friendships. We could confide in one another, and, when one of us felt emotion, whether good or bad, the rest of us felt it too: we were practically sisters. Amber's presence was comforting though. She sat in her usual position at the head of the table next to me with her cup of black coffee and a paper opened wide; her head dug into it. She liked coffee and the smell of it reminded me of her. I desperately wanted to swap my 100 kcal yogurt for her calorie free beverage! It was so frustrating. Diane was the nursing staff on that night. She was a short, fashionable looking woman and wore a white Rolex watch, which reminded me of my mum as she had a similar one. She sat at the opposite end of the table holding a straw up to Ellie's mouth, trying to poke it in!

"Come on Ellie, on the count of thwee. One, two, thwee..." Diane encouraged, but nothing happened. Ellie just sat there with a face as blank as a book staring into the wall opposite. Her legs shook and her bottom lip began to quiver.

"I know you can do it Ellie, you did it the other night for me." She said, stroking Ellie's hand and looking at her with sad eyes. Every few seconds she'd glance up at the rest of us over her spectacles that were perched on the end of her nose, to make sure we weren't doing anything we shouldn't have with our food. Diane had been there for years and knew all the tricks of the trade…well, except some of mine! Nothing got past Diane. In fact, I remember one supper time I had two rich tea biscuits to eat and I was not in a mind set to eat them. So, I thought I'd put my hiding skills to work. Quickly, whilst she was handing out everyone else's supper, I smuggled a whole biscuit up my cardigan sleeve and kept my head down, nibbling on the remaining one.

"That was quick Amy." Diane immediately noticed, giving me a very suspicious look up and down. I thought fast,

"My mum's ringing soon and I want to be finished." Diane gave me one last stare and continued with her surveillance of the table. I noticed her out of the corner of my eye peer under the table in my direction, and when she returned her head upright again, I gave her a cheeky smile.

"You haven't eaten that biscuit Amy have you?" Everyone looked at me.

"I have Diane, I promise I have." I exclaimed, and proudly turned my pockets inside out. She said okay, but I could tell she didn't believe me. After I'd finished I half ran back to my room and I had no choice other than to reluctantly stuff the hidden biscuit into my mouth and chew as fast as I could. And, as I'd expected, my bedroom door swung open a second later and Diane burst in.

"Where's that biscuit Amy?"

"I told you, I've eaten it Diane." I innocently replied. She searched me, peered under my bed and checked in the toilet. She bent over and held my hands,

"You pwomise me you ate it back there?"

"Yes", I lied. I had to lie. There was no other option.

"Because you know that you're here for us to help you get better. You're vewy poowly…"

"No I'm not!" I interrupted. I still didn't believe, or didn't want to believe, that I was too thin.

"You are darling, you just can't see it. Just please pwomise me you won't hide anything." I pretended to agree, and after a hug she turned to the door. She turned the handle but just before exiting turned to face me.

"It's not in your knickers is it?!"

"Diane!" I shrieked in a giggle.

"Just checking! I stayed put in the spot she'd left me in because I knew Diane; she'd come back into the room to check I wasn't disposing of it. And what a surprise: less than ten seconds after exiting she burst the door back open and I stood there smiling back at her; mischievously waving! I waited a few minutes before moving, then I took myself to the bathroom and frantically scraped any biscuit that was stuck into my teeth out of my mouth and down the toilet. I couldn't believe I'd eaten it. I'd promised myself I wouldn't. But if she'd caught me then that would've been it: she'd have reported back to the other staff and they'd have been aware of me struggling.

Barbara the advocate came to visit me the day after. She was a short, elderly, shriveled woman with sandy hair and glasses. She reminded me of a professor out of 'Harry Potter'! When she greeted me she had the most unusually deep voice for a woman; it was rather distracting to tell you the truth! Nevertheless, she was lovely and spent a good forty minutes talking to me. I told her my whole situation and stressed my need to get out of there. She sympathised with me and suggested lots of questions I could be asking Dr.Waissel in preparation for the tribunal, one of which was, 'What do you (Dr.Waissel) want from me?' She also gave me a list of solicitors I could contact to support my argument in the case. My dad would know who to pick, as he was one himself, and even though he disagreed with the whole tribunal arrangement, he respected my views and supported me anyway. After I'd gathered the relevant information and contacts I needed, I'd have to ring her again to arrange further planning. This whole process provided me with an inkling of hope and drove me to believe I was going to win.

The following day was my little sister's eighth birthday, and she was having a party in the 'Build a Bear workshop' at the Trafford Centre. Dr.Waissel and the other nurses had decided I wasn't allowed to attend as a lot of walking round the shops might have been involved, even though I'd already told them the party was only in one shop and the only walking required was round the corner to T.G.I Fridays for lunch. I was so upset about this. Family celebrations and get- togethers were extremely important to me and played a huge part in my determination to do well at college, as they were something I'd always looked forward to. Nevertheless, I didn't let this get in the way of me wishing Brooke a super birthday. I rang her up early in the morning, and I couldn't help but feel tearful when I heard her little excited voice over the phone and crinkling wrapping paper in the background. I missed watching her tear into tightly wrapped parcels and watching her face light up when she saw... the box it came in!

"I'll choose you a bear at the Bear Factory." She told me.

"Aw, Brooke, you don't have to."

"I want to." She replied. That was so sweet and I couldn't wait to see her after the party. Mum had arranged for herself, Brooke, Daniel, dad and grandad to visit me straight after the party so I could see Brooke on her birthday. I was really looking forward to seeing them all, but my OCD was really strong that day, causing my mood to fall and my concentration to switch to my hair.

"Look at you. You're hideous; you should be ashamed of your appearance. The weight is starting to show on your face Amy."

I'd been up since five o'clock trying to do my hair, but it just wouldn't go right. It didn't look the same as it had the previous day. I don't know what it was that told me it was right, but I know I had this feeling that I got that would make me feel okay with my hair. But until I got this feeling, I would never give up. I sat perched on the edge of my desk in front of the mirror with aching arms and a hot sweat running down my back. My head was becoming sore too with all the brushing and pulling and tugging. I'd get so mad I'd grab a clump of hair and yank it from my head, thinking I deserved the pain for being so ugly. To make matters even worse, the mirrors in the ward were like the wobbly ones you find in a fun house and I had to get right-up close to the mirror for me to see a non-distorted reflection. I'm sure they did this on purpose to disguise the amount of weight we were gaining and so we couldn't spend all day staring at our selves. This didn't stop me though. If I needed a reflection to do my hair in, I would get one. Even if that meant in the head of a spoon!

At each snack and meal, hospital assistants would shout me into the dining room with half finished hair. In a panic I'd tie the bobbles in a flurried rush and have to face everyone else in the dining room looking at me in a mess. I was so embarrassed and just wanted to go back to my mirror to sort myself out again. I really didn't want to eat any of the food given to me, as I felt really fat already without cramming more food in. But I had to eat it if I wanted to get back to my room.

My room became really hot and stuffy and my cheeks would begin to flush. I hated when they did this as it made me have a 'healthy glow', and I did not want to look healthy, because to me, healthy meant fat. I also changed my clothes numerous times to find something I'd look the least fat in. I'd flung all of my clothes, shoes and coats into heaps on my floor in a desperate hurry to find some clothes I would wear. I kept my eye on the alarm clock in the reflection of my mirror and as time ticked by, hour after hour, my heart pounced at the thought of my family turning up at the ward to find I was not ready. Eventually though at about half past two the ward's buzzer rang and I knew it was for me. I threw my brush to the floor in anger and moved away from my mirror. I scrambled through the mounds of clothing piled high on the floor and changed yet again to something that might feel more comfortable. Kelly came in and told me to hurry up, but I retreated to the mirror again and started messing. She opened the door a few minutes later and told me to go and see my family.

"But..." I began

"No Amy, they've come to see you; not to wait around. Out, now." So, reluctantly out I went, and there they were outside my door in the corridor. Brooke looked lovely. She had her party dress on and had her face painted as a white bunny and her hair was done all pretty too. My grandad was there as well: the first time I'd seen him since I had come in, which made me feel even more ashamed of letting anyone see me in the state I was in. Brooke came to me and pushed a cute bear in my face.

"This is for you." She said in a proud voice. The teddy was wearing a sash saying 'Get Well Soon', and this gesture made me feel really emotional. I didn't know what to say. I really wanted to put on a brave face just for her on her birthday, but I was feeling so low I just filled up.

"Oh Brooke, thank you, I love it." Then, quickly turning to my mum, "I hate it here. I'm so ugly mummy and it's not fair. I wanted to come to the party. I've had a dreadful day sat on my desk trying to do my hair and I hate it!" I burst out sobbing. Ushering me into the community room, my mum tried to calm me down in front of everyone; I could tell I was embarrassing her. As I cried I clutched my new teddy and slouched back into a chair, tucking my knees tightly to my chest. Several faint tear lines from earlier were getting washed away with the new rivers that were pouring from my eyes. Everything, the whole world just seemed like an empty hole with no purpose to it, and everyone seemed to be against me staying thin how I wanted. They were all out to get me.

"I've had it mummy. I don't want to be here anymore. I can't and I won't let them do this to me. I'm not eating anything. They can't do anything about it." My face turned red and shined from the wetness. I sat upright on my chair and clutched to its chair arm as if it had done something wrong to me. Out of the corner of my eye I could see my grandad trying to fight the tears. 'Oh no', I thought, I didn't want to make anyone upset, and this just made me worse. I just couldn't help letting my feelings out.

"It's your sister's birthday. Please try not to get so upset, especially today." My mum tried. The reality that I was probably ruining my sister's birthday had only just dawned on me, and the guilt of this made me sob even harder. Eventually

Michael called me in for afternoon snack. Brilliant! Just what I wanted. My family said they would wait for me whilst I ate it.

I stared at the floor and kept my eyes fixed on the orange they'd given me. I sat half turned away from everyone else with my head in my hands, sobbing. I heard whispers around the table.

"Are you okay, Amy?" Amber asked.

"Not really, no." I answered in a half whisper. Michael allowed me to have supervision with my family and had the cheek to tell them to keep me seated. As soon as he left the room I sprang from my seat in rebellion and walked round the room.

"Ha, I'm not doing anything they tell me to." I sniggered. The rest of the visit was a little quieter, as I'd used most of my energy up ranting and raving. When they went though, I slammed myself in my room and flung myself onto my desk again, to have one more attempt at fixing my hair.

Two days later it was Easter, and my mum, my dad and my sister came to see me. They had brought gifts too, (chocolate-free gifts!). My favourite present was a white fluffy bunny teddy holding a heart.

It really was a lovely visit. We pulled Easter crackers as well, and that time with my family almost felt normal.

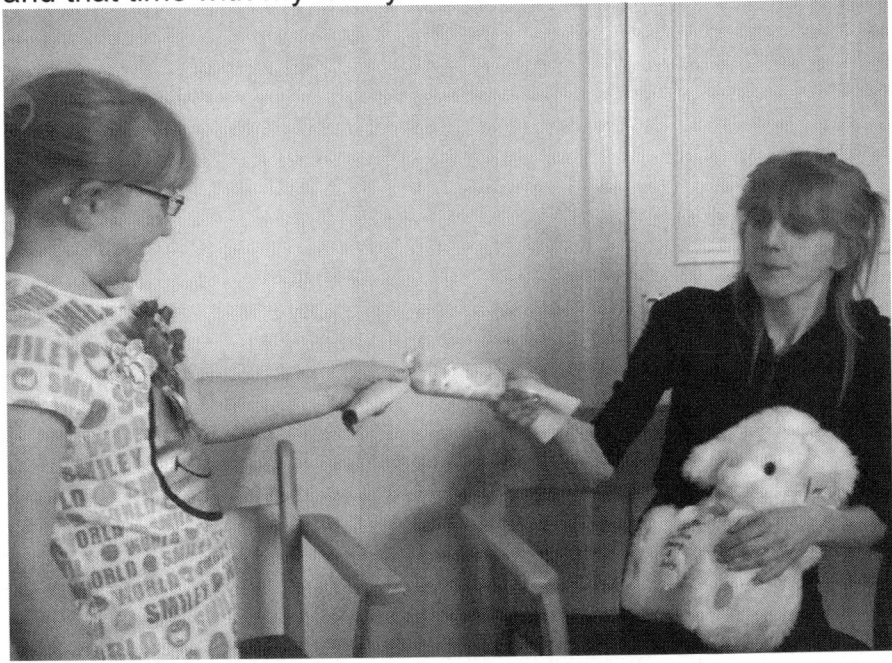

During the next couple of days, something had changed in Sharon. I couldn't quite put my finger on it but, something was definitely different. She seemed focused on something all of a sudden and distanced herself from the rest of us. It all came clear though at one tea time when she marched in proudly carrying a plate of beans on toast. I couldn't believe it. I'd never seen Shannon eat solid food before! Was she really going to eat it? Would she manage it? A funny sort of butterfly sensation fluttered about in my stomach and I began to feel all 'motherly', as if I was someone for her to look up to. I thought she'd approach it really slowly and take timid little bites, but astonishingly she ate quite quickly and I felt so proud of her. I saw Ellie out of the corner of my eye look to Sharon in an admiral way and hoped that Sharon would be a good role model for her, as she and Ellie always supported each other through everything.

"Do ya remember when the last time I was in, and they called me cornflake girl? Cos I had cornflakes for breakfast, cornflakes for dinner and cornflakes for tea!" Sharon announced, half chewing a piece of toast and bean juice gathering in the corners of her mouth. "Yeah, they don't let us do that no more cos now it's an all eating disorders unit." A few months back the ward had been for any mental illness, whether that was an eating disorder or a behavioral disorder or whatever.

"Aw, I would have been thankful to have been allowed just cereal all day!" I thought. How unfair was that, when we were presented with three course meals and all the trimmings?

With new ward rounds, (and weight gain of course), came new privileges. My first sort of 'reward' was to have longer walks to the end of the road and back. The second was shorter supervision times and eventually I worked up to being able to make my own snacks and preparing the things that went with my meals. And oh yes! That meant one thing: I could give myself less food than I was supposed to… if I was sneaky that is, as we were watched like hawks by a member of staff at all times. At first I found this really difficult to get away with because there was no single time when we were left alone. But as I got used to where the staff would stand and how I could distract them, things became easier for me. The first thing I got away with was my albran and milk. Whilst talking to the member of staff on supervision, I'd scrunch my hand inside the cereal packet just before emptying into the bowl and deposit a handful into my dressing gown pocket. As for the milk, I learnt this tip off Sharon and it was really easy; why hadn't I thought of it myself? Once I'd washed out the measuring jug under the tap, I left a couple of centimeters of water lurking in the bottom so that I didn't have to measure as much milk out. This also worked quite well for apple juice too!

"Nooooooo!" I couldn't help but scream at the top of my voice after the dietician had exited the room. "Not another diet increase! I can't deal with any more food!" Now I was eating loads. For breakfast I was now to have one portion of cereal with milk, a large banana, a slice of toast with margarine and jam, and 300 ml of fruit juice. This was more than anybody else had to eat and I felt really hard done by for being given the largest diet. In my own mind, it felt like a sign that I was the most ill as I required the most calories to put weight on, but I knew that wasn't the case.

That was it. Plan B had to be put into operation. A sneaky handful of albran and a little milk hidden here and there was no way near enough to save me from the extra calories. I had to think of something else, and fast. Kelly used to stand over me whilst I spread the fat and sugar onto the burnt pieces of toast in front of me. I had put just less than half of one of those individual margarine tubs onto it and was in the process of throwing it away when Kelly intervened.

"Err, no. The whole tub please." She said in a raised voice.

"What, all of it? Every last bit?"

"Yes. That's one standard portion." She replied. 'Yeah, one standard portion for a greedy American maybe!' I thought. I scraped the rest of it onto my knife and reluctantly, scrunching my nose, spread it on top. Kelly took the empty tub, lifted the lid to have an inspection and threw it away. The toast was a tricky food to dispose of in the kitchen, but I soon found ways around this. Now and again the supervisor's attention would fall on something else, like getting their own breakfast ready, or answering to another patient, and I took these golden opportunities whenever I was lucky enough to get one. I'd make sure to make my toast next to the microwave so then when I had the margarine on my knife it would be easy to wipe off under it. It worked like a treat, but I held my breath every time I did it and my heart pounded a million times a minute as I prayed for it not to fall from the bottom of the microwave onto the side. A few times when the nurses were getting the trays from the kitchen to take into the dining room, I noticed from outside the door that the big blob of margarine had fallen from its hiding place and I panicked through all of breakfast hoping with all my might that no one would notice it. Straight after, I'd rush to the office with my microwavable teddy and a tissue, (supposed to be for my nose), and ask if I could heat him up. They supervised me of course, but when they weren't looking I lowered the tissue from my 'apparently' runny nose and wiped up the margarine.

   I'd always wear these almost knee length high black boots with my leggings and at the table; in between a nibble here and a nibble there, would place a big chunk of toast and jam into the mouth of my boot, then flush it down the toilet afterwards. (In fact, the jammy stains are still here as I'm writing this recollection!) I tried to do this as discretely as I could, as I didn't want the other patients to see incase I was giving them a bad example. But Ellie saw now and again and I just eyed her as if to say 'please don't say anything.' She never did say anything; she was on my side and was just as eager to get rid of calories as I was. However, not everyone kept quiet. Now that Sharon had decided to 'get on with the program' to get out of there, she gradually stopped taking part in our little plans to exercise and dispose of food. Instead, she decided to snitch on me when I was at one of my desperate moments. My diet plan specifically stated that I was to have 'lightly spread' margarine on my sandwiches, as I had a dislike of this slop that some people considered a delicacy! And the majority of the time my sandwiches came choc-a-block full with this lumpy, yellow lard. No way was I going to let that greasy fat slither down my throat and onto my thighs! So, (like anyone with an ounce of respect for their personal health), I wiped it off with my fingers onto the cling film the sandwiches came wrapped in, which was scrunched tightly in my fist. 'Now here we have one invention more worthwhile than the wheel', I thought, "two uses for the price of one: great for transporting things *and* a perfect hiding place for unwanted crap!' But my heart skipped a beat when I saw Sharon glance up darkly at me from her tuna sandwich; she gave the nurse a nudge and pointed in my direction. I pretended not to notice her and began to pick up my sandwich properly. After a pause I began wiping the bread again and Amanda told me to go out of the room with her.

"I know what you're going to say." I immediately told her when we were outside. "It's about me wiping margarine off, I know! And do you want to know what else I know? I know that Sharon is the one who grassed me up!"

"Amy, you know not to do that. The chefs in the kitchen know what a proper portion is, so what you get you ha...."

"But Sharon does it! I've seen her!" I couldn't help but interrupt.

"Well if we see her doing it we will tell her as well" was the stern reply. But before turning back into the dining room I muttered to myself, "Well the chef butters bread like he's cementing a wall!"

"Pardon?" she asked in a low voice.

"Nothing!" I answered. I couldn't believe it. I just couldn't believe it; Sharon of all people. She was my friend, or so I thought she was. A cold drift came between us for a while and now it was twice as hard to get away with anything.

Despite having being caught hiding food, I was still eligible to go on the next recreation, as I had continued to gain weight at a steady rate, and I was dead excited to know where we would be going. It was decided in ward round that we would visit 'The Blue Planet Aquarium'. I loved it there and had been many a time with my family. However, the ward round wasn't all pleasant. Sharon was sat at the opposite side of the room giving me the evils, so I kindly returned them. There was an awkward atmosphere and I think everyone could tell something was up. I didn't like falling out and the bad mood it put me in made me even more resentful about eating. But the worst thing was that Ellie, who was hunched over in the chair next to her, seemed to be blanking me, and I knew that

Sharon had said something. This was awful. One of the only things getting me through this nightmare was the close friendships I had made in there; especially with Ellie and Emily. Without these, I don't think I could have found the strength to battle my fears of food. I hoped we were still friends.

"Does anyone else have anything to say?" Emily quietly asked as she was about to close the meeting.

"Yes actually, I have something to say." Sharon quickly answered, and she began, whilst day-dreamishly staring at the floor in front of her. "There are a few people," she glanced up at me, "who are putting the rest of us off wanting to get better and it's not fair what they are doing."

"Would you like to reiterate Sharon?" Fay asked in deep concentration on the matter.

"What I mean is", she continued, "is that some people want to get better, but when they are trying to eat whilst others are hiding or getting rid of food, it puts the rest of us off and to tell you the truth, it's really fucking annoying me!"

"Language Sharon." Natasha reminded with a crinkled brow and a stern expression on her face. There was a long silence, and the odd shuffle of bums on squeaky chairs. I could tell the staff weren't impressed with Sharon's blunt and disrespectful manner of expressing herself, but judging from the wave of nodding heads, I knew they agreed with her point.

After a painstakingly long lecture from the staff, we were allowed to exit and I watched in horror as Sharon led Ellie, arm in arm, down the corridor, whispering as they went. I was so annoyed. I just wanted to cry, so I turned back into the community room where Eliza was still sauntering, and told her that I was the target of what Sharon had just said and that she was leading Ellie to believe I was no use as a friend. She comforted me and offered to come back to my room for a chat.

I really liked Eliza. She was a really caring and fun loving person who always wanted to help. She and I had therapy sessions together on a weekly basis and during these times with her, I felt as though I could tell her almost anything. In a way, her giddy and exciting personality made me feel as though she was my elder sister. In fact, before I had reached my first goal of BMI 14, she promised me she would take me out to a local 'George' shop clothes shopping once I'd reached that, and she did. It was a really girly day out and, for that period of time, I actually forgot I was in the hospital. We looked at all the clothes I loved to wear: the kiddie's clothes, (as they were the ones I could fit into.) I really wanted to buy another pair of skinny jeans, as I felt my current ones were beginning to feel a bit clingy. However, I was adamant that I was not to buy a size bigger; just a different fit so they didn't show as much fat. In my mind buying a bigger size was physical evidence of my weight gain, and I would not allow myself to outgrow my small clothes. I soon found a really nice pair of denim drain pipe jeans and rushed, although minding not to run, to the fitting rooms. I grabbed the curtain and yanked it shut, and then faced the full length mirror in front of me, frowning at my huge legs. My heart felt a sinking sensation, so I started to mess with my hair as a sort of means for an escape. After a while though, Eliza called me and I quickly shoved the jeans on and stuck my head through the curtain. I wouldn't step out though; I was far too embarrassed to expose my expanding body. After painstakingly staring up and down at my legs however, I decided to buy them. They weren't the nicest, most complementary pants in the world, but anything was better than what I was quickly out-growing.

As we queued up to pay I watched the other customers: mums hand in hand with their young children; groups of teenage chavs in scruffy school uniforms slurping juice from the bottom corners of cartons; babies in prams innocently shaking their rattles, and I thought to myself how nobody there would have had a clue what I was going through. To them, that afternoon spot of shopping probably seemed like boring routine, but to me at that moment in time, it felt like a breath of fresh air and a taste of freedom. If only I could have stayed in the shop all day long.

When we got back I had to have snack. Everyone was curious to know what I'd bought. Honestly, you'd have thought I'd been away to a foreign country for a fortnight, "Did you have a good time?"

"What did you get…anything for me?" They all asked in unison. I tried not to sound too exhilarated as I didn't want to make the others feel bad for not having the chance to come. So my answer was, "Yeah, it was good. Got some jeans!"

Before the next recreation, I decided there was only one thing to do. And that was to approach Sharon and apologise- even though I didn't know what I was saying sorry for. I just wanted to be friends again. Ellie was with her sauntering outside the alcove in the corridor.

"Can we be friends? I don't like falling out. I'm sorry." I offered, and Sharon, after a pause, accepted. We shook hands, and I gave them both a hug and hurried off to my room to hide my joy at making-up. Hopefully this would make things easier to cope with whilst in the ward environment.

The morning of recreation came and I was in my room, again, tying my bobbles; frantically trying to get my hair right. I was so annoyed I couldn't do it; especially when I was going to be seen in public. It was almost as if the demon living inside of me wanted me locked away from everyone else. He didn't like me to relax or have fun. *'Going to have a good day out are we? No you're not. Not if I have anything to do with it. You don't deserve to.'* We had three minutes before we left and being all flustered I threw myself onto my bed and cried with frustration. I heard a knock on my door and Moira popped her head in to get me.

"I'm not going." I told her; one hand still on my head holding the piece of hair I hadn't managed to tie correctly.

"Why ever not?" She asked.

"I'm just not. I'm staying here."

"Oh no you don't. You're going with the others, now come on they're leaving."

"No!" I retaliated.

"Well if you don't go you are *not* staying in your room. I'll lock it and you'll sit outside with the rest of us." Now this, for me, was not an option. I had to stay in my room by myself so I could finish my hair, but I knew she wouldn't let me.

"Please?" I tried. But no was the answer. So in a huff I tied my bobble as quickly as I could and slouched out of my room.

All the way there I kept quiet, staring at my ugly reflection in the window. Even when we arrived I still had only my hair on my mind, and in the toilets I fiddled with it more. When we entered the aquarium though, the glistening aqua blue tanks seemed to dilute my problems. Turtles soared through the water whilst some bathed lazily on the sandy banks above them. Colourful scales that shimmered like stars shone from the elegant backs of angel fish, and tiny orange crabs scuttled clumsily along the tank beds. My mind wandered from these exotic creatures to the rainbow coral that lined the sand. 'What would it be like to roam free: no rules, no sections, no diet plan?' Those fish didn't know what they'd got. I'd have given anything to be one of them, and I could imagine me shrinking; gills sinking their way into the flesh on my neck and fins sprouting where my arms would have been. And then came that wonderful image of me darting off into the open water away from the hell I was trapped in behind the glass. Just as I was creating this sensational idea in my head, Ellie grabbed my arm and pulled me to a huge circular tank in the centre of the room. Flat fish exposed their soft, slimy backs above the water as they floated round. I hovered my hand above them and carefully tickled their backs. They were unexpectedly rough and bumpy. One jerked suddenly and splashed water over the edge of the tank. This made me laugh! The rebel! In another room, microscopic frogs of all different colours and patterns sprang around humid, leafy tanks, camouflaging themselves into the surrounding greenery. They sort of reminded me of myself in the hospital: changing themselves in correspondence to the situations they were faced with.

　　Just before I thought I was having a time too good to be true, we had to have snack. Kelly led us to some benches situated round the corner from where the shark show was held and handed round the snacks. I had to have my apple juice stored inside a Fortijuice bottle, which I wasn't too impressed about. The thought of all those calories from the Fortijuice spreading into my apple drink from off the insides of the bottle made me shudder. Groups of young school children, being lead by their teachers, passed by us in a line. I wished I was one of them too, the lucky sprites! After snack we were allowed to stand on the moving floor that passed through a glass tunnel underneath the water. Humongous sharks with pointy teeth the size of nails sauntered majestically above our heads, whilst in the distant, murky water, brave scuba divers fed the hungry monsters. Ellie made me laugh: instead of standing still on the moving platform that did all the work for you, she walked by the side of it on the proper carpeted floor…mmm, I wonder why?! I followed suit. Whilst on the subject of exercise, Ellie and I ran round the outdoor play area, which was actually meant for little kids, like lunatics swinging from bars and sliding down poles! It was great fun but didn't last long when we caught Michael's eye.

In the last ten minutes we explored the gift shop in search for interesting bits to buy. I found this gooey; rubber frog filled with slime that splatted when thrown against a wall! I thought it was dead cool so I bought it for my sister and a chameleon pen that made a sound and lit up for myself. The car ride back was better than the one arriving. I'd realised that having a break from doing my hair actually did me good and that I didn't have to have perfect hair in order to have a good time.

Over the following couple of days, emotions ran high. Lizzie was discharged. We didn't want her leave; she was a part of the 'family' and it was really difficult to let go. I felt like I'd known her for years, not a few months, and what made things worse was we had also been informed that a new patient was to arrive on the ward any day soon. He was a boy: the only one out of all of us. We dreaded a new patient, for they were likely to be thinner than us as they hadn't received any treatment yet. I couldn't cope when someone around me was thinner than I was. I *had* to be the thinnest one. It was non negotiable. Terrible skinny images of a scrawny little lad filled my head and an envious emotion took over me. Ellie looked like a frightened kitten and became quiet for a while, which was highly unlike her. One night at supper we gathered around the dining table and discussed our views about the new comer.

"I hate it when this happens." Ellie told us, her chin in her hands. "I've been here that long that I've seen patient after patient come and go from the ward and every time it just gets harder to cope with." I'd just realised that Ellie had gone through this many a time and must have been fed up with it. I felt sorry for her. I became shaky, shy and uneasy and I now understood why Ellie looked so timid on that first night she met me. I was going through the same as she had when I'd entered the ward.

"It's horrible." Sharon added. "But I'm not gonna let it bother me. I'm here to get better and no new, skinny kid is gonna stop me from doing that." For once I agreed with Sharon, but I still couldn't help but feel apprehensive. Emily just sat opposite me with a blank expression on her face. Maybe she had other issues on her mind, or maybe her fortisip was becoming a little overwhelming.

"I hate it too" admitted Amber, gently blowing the steam which was rising from her cup of coffee. "It's just another obstacle that comes in the way of our recovery." But I didn't want to recover, as recovering meant putting weight on and becoming 'normal'. I had the stay thin, I just had to. Despite all our reasons for not wanting anyone else on the ward, we were all slightly excited about the thought of having male company. One of us might have had the chance to get a boyfriend! It was also a strange thought that the new comer was a boy. You don't hear of as many cases of anorexia in males. I wonder if this made it even harder for him: not to be understood by the majority of outsiders. Or maybe it made him more proud of the fact that he was one of the few skinny lads around. It made me less worried though, knowing he was the opposite sex, as it would have been harder to compare myself to a boy than it would to another girl.

The next night, things got too much and hit new heights and I just had to get out of there. I sauntered in the hall way of the unit glaring at the tiny, blurred writing in the visitor's book through my water filled eyes; wondering what I'd done to deserve this. My breathing was fast and interrupted; I was choking on my breath. The whole situation: the hospital; gaining weight; missing college, friends and family; saying bye to Lizzie; a new patient... the lot, just became overwhelming and I wasn't prepared to take anymore of that crap.

"Hey, what's up?" offered a popular nurse from next door.

"Evvvrrryythinnng!" I snapped through clenched teeth, refusing to lift my eyes from the book.

" Ahh, come on, things will get better, you'll see. I've seen loads of patients like you who, at the end of their stay here look back and think, 'why was I worrying so much?'"

"And that's where you're wrong." I looked up and stared her in the eyes. "You, and all the nurses here and everyone, you think you know how I feel. Well you know summit? You don't! People seem to think that, 'oh, she's just another *typical* anorexic, I know how she's feeling; I can talk her round, I've read it in books!' when actually, you might want to consider that everyone is different. I'm not like anybody else, and I know that this isn't the right place for me. But no one understands that do they?"

"But…"

"I just want to go home where I belong." I interrupted. "That's all!" I thumped my elbows down on the shelf and plunged my face into my hands. The nurse stood and watched as heavy tears poured from my eyes and rolled down my cheeks, leaving shiny trails as they went. She left me alone.

Meanwhile, hand-over to the night staff had just finished in the community room and the nurses piled out from the door at the top of the corridor. I quickly slipped myself behind the patient payphone door, which was inside a dark alcove in the wall and waited for them to, one by one, exit the ward. I was going to attempt to escape. The ward's door locked when it closed and only opened with a protected buzzer available to the staff only, so I had to figure out a way to lodge something between the door and the wall to prevent it from closing completely; then I'd slip out later. I rummaged inside my pockets and, along with the gritty crumbs of old food, found a packet of tissues. The door clicked open. I ran from behind the door, slid across the carpet and tried to wedge the tissues in the gap. But the door was too heavy and quickly closed. I thrust the packet to the floor and stamped on it. Sharon and the other patients had witnessed this and came to comfort me.

"Amy, there's no use tryin' to escape, right." assured Sharon. "This is my second admission to the ward now, and I

know more than most that runnin' away just gets you into deeper shit! You'll get all your privileges taken off ya, put on a one to one, banned from rec and unable to go out of the ward," she stared at me hard and continued, "which means no home leave, and no chance of discharge." Taking all of this into consideration, I was here anyway and was going to gain weight if I tried to stop it or not, so I had nothing to lose but to try. If I didn't try, I'd never know for sure what would happen. So, I lifted the flap of the 'emergency exit' handle which unlocked all the doors, then…
'BLEEEEEEEEP BLEEEEEP BLEEE…', The emergency alarm shrieked its shrill voice through the whole hospital. "Shit!" I let go and legged it into my room, slamming the door behind me. Luckily no one suspected it was me, so I got away with that one.

The morning after, we received ward round and I was allowed to go home for the weekend, which meant I could go to my brother's 15th birthday party. But to shatter the good news, we were informed in a special community meeting that the new patient would be arriving. Whispers and anxious looks were exchanged throughout the morning and over lunch too.

"I wonder what he's like?", "How old is he?", and "How thin do ya reckon he is?"… Then, "I bloody hope he's fit!" Blurted out Ellie… honestly, trust *her*! We all heard the front buzzer sound whilst having lunch, and my stomach turned a somersault… and not for the food! He was here. The dining room door was shut and we were left with Amanda, who was staring at me from opposite, trying to urge me to eat my food, which I was blatantly ignoring as I was not in the mood. My hair had not gone right, again, so I had pulled a baker boy hat over my head to hide under. I didn't like wearing hats as I didn't want to get used to them being an every day essential; I could imagine me as an old aged pensioner shrivelled beneath a hat shaped like a tea-cosy! They were useful for concealing mischievous eye gestures though!

We didn't see the new patient all day. He was lead to Lizzie's old room with Michael and I couldn't help but hold a grudge against the thought that someone else was taking over Lizzie's room. At snack we were all seated as usual, when the door was pushed open and a small, short boy shuffled in, hands in pockets, head hidden in a black rimmed beanie hat and dark eyes on the floor. He wore a full black, baggy tracksuit complete with a tracksuit coat. I thought he was rather cute. You could just about see his brown hair poking out from beneath the back of his hat like a little pony tail, and he had small, defined features. I couldn't quite make out how skinny his frame was, as it was hidden under the loose clothing. He perched himself on a chair at the end of the table; his feet dangling above the floor, and was handed a yogurt. 'Would he eat it?' I wondered. 'How bad was his condition?' To my surprise, he peeled back the lid and made a start. A slow one, but it was a start. He licked the yogurt off the spoon how a puppy might lick an ice cream.

"Hey I'm Amy, what's your name?"

"Max." He muttered.

"How old are you?" asked Ellie shyly.

"Fourteen." He didn't seem a man of many words, but, pleasant enough, although I was envious of losing my title of 'the new patient', as that took away from me the thought that I was the most ill; the thinnest.

Later that day my dad arrived to pick me up for home leave.

"Where you goin?" asked Max, whilst sat on the sofa in the lounge.

"Home. You'll get to soon. See ya Sunday, mate." He nodded; I hugged everyone else and left.

Daniel was so pleased to have me home for his party. We were going to the Trafford centre to play crazy golf with our family and friends, then to 'TGI Fridays' for tea. Everyone looked lovely at the party, and I was the only ugly one there, hiding under a brim; concealing my eyes, which were a dark, stormy colour. Nevertheless, I did my best to hide my feelings, as not to ruin Dan's day.

Golf was great. The soothing, exotic sounds of rainforest animals echoed from speakers situated in secret crevices within the tropical themed course, which relaxed me slightly and softened the emotional rollercoaster I was riding through my mind. But, the more I tried to forget about the situation I was in, the more I couldn't help thinking about it. I had chosen to wear a strappy top so I could still see my thin arms. It made me feel better knowing that I was still thinner than everyone else around me.

After the game we went to the restaurant just around the corner, and my true feelings began to set in whilst we were all sat round the table. For a long time now, I'd had strong feelings and urges to run away from the hospital. I'd dream up the perfect plan in my room at night, (the only real time I had to think to myself), and play it over and over in my head, making sure every detail was immaculately thought out. Nothing else was working: hiding food wasn't preventing me from gaining weight; 'playing the game' wasn't getting me anywhere; refusing food was never going to work; so running away from the problem seemed like the only solution. The only thing stopping me from taking action was the effect it would have on my family and friends and the strong disadvantage that would play against me when my tribunal eventually took place. Everyone would be devastated and ever so worried about me. I couldn't put them through any more stress than they were already experiencing. However, when I felt my thighs and expanding legs under the table, the agony of gaining weight over-ruled anything and everything else. The only thing that mattered was that I stayed thin. The way I saw it was, 'I'd rather be unhealthy and happy for the rest of my life, than healthy and unhappy.' I sat there quietly; glancing round at everyone with bright spirits, chatting happily to one another, not having a clue what was circling around in my mind. When I get all emotional, I start to visualise and sort of re-live treasured memories. Like past holidays we'd had together, birthdays, Christmases...these all contributed to the side of me that was preventing my thoughts from becoming reality. My eyes filled up at the thought the devastation would do to my parents and a sinking sensation plummeted deep into the centre of my stomach.

    The end of the party was near and I had come to the extremely difficult conclusion that I would run away from the hospital. I had to. It was the only way to get my point across and prove to everyone that this hospitalization process was not working and was never going to. Saying goodbye to my mum, before my dad took me back, was heartbreaking. Of course, she didn't feel the same way as she had no idea she might not see me again. I still remember my words as clear as crystal.

"Bye mummy, I love you so much and I always will do. You always remember that." My mum looked at me suspiciously as if to say, 'this isn't the last time we'll see each other you know!' Then she paused and asked me,

"You're not running off are you?" I gulped back my tears and crossed my fingers, swearing I'd never do anything like that. But I couldn't tell her the truth. They'd contact the hospital and have me on a constant one to one, and that meant definite weight gain, plus no freedom. "Right," she continued, "Because I'd never forgive you for that." This really hurt. I'd lose everything: everything, and my mum, all to keep my thinness. This is just how hypnotised my demon had me. I felt so strongly about staying thin that nothing else in the whole world mattered. I'd do just about anything to keep hold of it.

That night, I planned to leave it a few days before I ran away, as I didn't want to ruin the birthday spirit that was still in the air. 'A few more pounds won't make a difference,' I thought, 'I'll just lose it all quickly when I run off anyway. Still, I packed a little rucksack: paper, pens, stamps, an address book, tissues, money, an inhaler...all the essentials; so then when the perfect moment came I could swipe the bag and leg it.

The day came. I didn't know it was the day, it just sort of happened. The right opportunity came and I was in no position not to take it. We were all supposed to go to support group, but I claimed I wasn't feeling well and asked for my mobile 'to text my mum', and so I was allowed to stay in my room by myself. The others slouched up to the community room.

"Pssst," I whispered to Ellie, from behind my bedroom door, who was trailing behind everyone else, "Ellie, I'm gonna go."

"You what?" she asked, eyes wide open.

"I'm going to run Ellie, I have to. Please don't tell anyone, I just need to go."

"What, now? How?"

"The door's unlocked right?" she nodded, "I'll just leg it when I get the chance and won't stop till it's safe."

"Oh please look after yourself Amy." She gave me a squeeze.

"I will, just promise you'll distract anyone from checking on me for as long as you can okay?" I waited three minutes, grabbed my jacket and bag, and then opened my door as quietly as I could. Muffled voices were coming from behind the staff room door. I knew the staff were all inside, and the coast was clear. I prayed no one would come out, and after a short pause, as I thought about what I was about to do and the consequences of it, I sprinted as lightly as I could across the corridor, shoved my hand onto the green button which opened the ward door and ran down the stairs. My heart was pounding a million beats per minute. What if they'd heard me? 'Ah, too late now' I thought. It felt as though it was going to burst out of my chest. All I remember of my descent down the stairs was a big blurry spiral flying past my eyes. A cleaner happened to be brushing near the entrance so I slowed down for a second, as not to look suspicious, then ran faster than I had ever done in my entire life out the main door and up the drive. It was a huge, huge risk what I was doing. Any one of the staff from the hospital could have been passing outside at any time, and the only moving figure along the driveway was me. And what made things worse was that the staff room window overlooked the whole drive, so if they glanced out I would've been spotted and chased! I got to the top of the drive and turned a sharp right down a narrow overgrown mud path leading into the woods at the back of the hospital. This was scary enough in itself for I hated wasps and probably disturbed a few nests whilst fighting my way through the protruding nettle bushes. Leaves and twigs rustled and snapped beneath my feet and I glanced back every few seconds, almost expecting to see a member of staff gaining on me. But there was none in sight. 'I wonder if they even know I'm missing yet.' A hot sweat trickled down my back. I hoped not!

The pathway seemed to go on forever and ever, but soon I saw light in the distance, which made me run even harder. I came to an opening where a few humongous cottages were built. I darted through that, pulling my hat back securely onto my head, and down a further pathway that connected. I'd never gone that far before. We were only allowed so far on our walks and I didn't even know if it was a dead end or not. The pathway began to slope and opened and became rocky under my feet. It was an opening to the woods and I knew there must have been an escape route through there. I never stopped; not once, not until I was far enough away.

Eventually, two elderly ladies walking their dogs approached in my direction from down a steep cobbled slope ahead. I smiled casually at them, wiping off the sweat that sparkled across my face with my jacket sleeve.

"Hello", I gestured. "Nice day isn't it?"

"Why, yes deary it is. Where are you off to then?" The shorter of the two asked. Thinking on the spot, I replied, "Erm, I'm going to see my grandma."

"Be careful on your own won't you. It's a bit quiet round here." The other offered. This made me feel a little uneasy. I hated being on my own in my own home; never mind in an unfamiliar wood. But I bid her I would, and then we parted. It was a slippy climb up the cobbles as it had rained hard the night before, and my shoes were covered in mud. I kept going and going until the wood ended and lead onto a side road in the middle of Altrincham, somewhere.

What had I done? They must have noticed I was missing by now; it'd been a good forty minutes at least. As much as I regretted running away, the more freedom I felt and the fears of weight seemed to drift away slightly. I ran over and over my situation and the best next steps to take, and to be honest, I didn't know what to think, where to go, who to talk to. I was scared. But god-damn grateful I wasn't in that hell hole anymore. Just as I was wondering-off into a daze my phone rang. 'Should I answer it?' What if it was the hospital?

"H-hello" I stammered.

"Hiya super star!" It was my dad. Phew, was I glad to hear from him! He was at work and was just checking up on me. We started to chat casually, but I couldn't concentrate on a word he was saying to me. The guilt was too much. I had to tell him.

"Dad", I murmured, "I'm not at the hospital."

"What do you mean you're not at the hospital? Where are you?"

"I can't tell you Daddy, or you'll take me back." Why had I told him? I'd made the perfect get away and then went and blew my cover! "I wish I could tell you Daddy, but I'm not going back to that place." My Dad paused for a moment; I don't think it had quite absorbed- this revelation.

"Are you with someone?" He asked.

"No, I'm by myself, it's just me. No one knows I'm gone. Please don't tell them. I just needed to tell you because, beca... well...err.., I dunno, I just needed to tell someone." Even though I couldn't see my Dad, I knew his face would have been a sickly worried expression by the long silence in between his speech.

"Well what are you going to do? Where are you going?"

"I'm going to go somewhere... away, or come home. But if I do come home please promise never to take me back there again." I pleaded.

"Amy, you know I can't promise that. You're on a section of the mental health act and there is nothing we can do, even if we wanted to." This news broke my heart and I bursed into tears. The thought that my plan might fail came into my mind and that just wasn't an option for me.

"Then I'm not coming home Daddy. Ring Dr.Waissel and tell her to let me go or I'm never coming back!" It choked me to say these words, but I felt so strongly about freeing myself from that prison and force-feeding routine that I would risk going away from my family.

"Where are you, Amy?" He persisted in asking, but I wouldn't tell him. My mum was in a state of her own at home and I pleaded him not to tell her where I was in case it made her worse, but he said he had to and told me he'd ring me back once he'd told her. "And stay safe." He added.

'Now what?" I thought. I just kept walking. That's all I could do. Eventually I got to a main road and came upon a man whom seemed to know his way around Altrincham... if that was where I still was! So I thought I'd use my initiative and ask him for directions.

"Excuse me, erm, would you happen to know the way to Altrincham met station please?" Thankfully the man said yes, and directed me in the general direction. He walked part of the way, as he was heading that way too. He, as well as the elderly ladies, asked where I was going, and I gave him the same reply, "I'm going to my grandma's, but I've never been by myself before, and I don't live around here you see." He seemed to buy my alibi, but as he chatted to me, all I seemed to take-in was that his mouth was moving and noises were coming out. I don't remember one bit more that the man said to me; my mind was all over the place and it hurt me to think about it.

My phone rang again when I reached my destination. It was my mum.

"Where are you?" she asked in a soft, surprisingly calm voice.

"Oh, mummy I'm so sorry. I didn't mean to run off, I just had to. And I'm sorry. I'm sorry. I love you!" Tears rolled down my face and onto the low brick wall I was leaning on outside the met station. I tried to cover my face from the passing high school students as I spoke but I couldn't conceal my emotions.

"Help me Mummy." I begged.

"I can't believe you have done this to me."

"I haven't done this to *you*", I love you, and I'm running away from those horrible doctors and stupid, stupid laws, not you, never you." I started to cry harder. I was attracting a few unwanted glances too.

"Please tell me where you are." She asked again, resisting the tears.

"Okay, but only if you promise not to tell the nurses." She agreed and I let-on.

"I'm at Altrincham met station." I confessed.

"How did you get there?"

"I dunno, I just walked and walked through these woods and then asked a man and he told me. Don't be worried about me; I'm fine; I'm sensible enough."

"Well where are you going to go?" She asked.

"Anywhere," I told her, "anywhere that they can't find me. I was going to come home but Daddy said you'd have to take me back."

"If you did come home I can't promise anything, but I know what I want, and I want my daughter back at home with me. I'll see what we can do, but come home first eh?" I knew she was trying to persuade me to come home, whatever the result, but I just couldn't, not if it wasn't definite I'd be allowed to leave the hospital. All my efforts to resist treatment had to pay-off for something, it just *had* to. She kept me on the phone for half an hour, and by this time my face was streaming with tears and my cheeks were red and flushed.

"Right," I announced finally, "I'm going to go now."

"No don't go," my mum chipped-in suddenly, "W-wait a minute, I need to talk to you!" I thought this was a tad fishy how she was trying to keep me on the phone and I could here dampened voices in the back ground, but I thought nothing of it at the time. I just thought it was the tv or something. The next thing I knew, I was trying to find a met, when I spotted July, the ward manager, out of the corner of my eye, and then sal, (a nurse from downstairs), rushing frantically from behind her; looking in all directions.

'OH CRAP!' They'd found me. "What's happened?" My mum asked down the phone.

"Oh no, Mummy, they've found me, they've got me. Help me Mummy."

"Who's got you?"

"July from the ward."

"Do you know her?"

"Yes. Please help me mummy, please help me." I tried to discretely turn around and sneak back the other way, but they caught a glimpse of my hat. I started to peg it when they both came at me at once and secured me tightly by my arms. July took the phone from my hands and reassured my mum I was safe, and then they escorted me to a car that was waiting at the entrance to the station.

"Do you know who's been out for the past hour and a half worried sick searching for you?" July asked me in a stern voice.

"No." I answered in a ticked-off tone.

"Fay." She replied. I couldn't believe it. Fay had actually spent time worrying about *me*! I didn't think I was worth worrying over. I felt really awful for worrying her and I was really disappointed in myself for breaking her trust in me. As soon as I saw her face from inside the car, I felt so ashamed, but angry that my plan hadn't worked. I refused to say a word; I only used paralinguistics to communicate. They put me in the back seat of the car and I leant my face against the door all the way back. This was the worst feeling ever: defeat, fear, disappointment, worry, helplessness, and despair. What was I to do?

Fay pulled into the car park and let me out, although remained within arms reach at all times. Slumping up the staircase I'd fled down earlier, I felt sick at the thought of what they'd do next. They took me down the corridor and into the community room. The other patients were having snack in the dining room and when I passed they all turned, leaving soft, muffled whispers lurking behind me. I sat on a chair opposite Fay, keeping my eyes glued on my feet. Fay took my bag and searched it. She told me to remove my shoes and socks and pull my pockets inside out, just in case I had something sharp on me! (Like I would!)

"I know you have a problem about removing your hat once you've done your hair Amy, but we really need to check under it." Fay said in a soft voice with a crinkled brow. I was in no mood to argue, so I slowly, but reluctantly took it off and turned my face to the side so they didn't see how ugly I was without a hat to cover me up! Once the check was done, I was led to my room where a police officer came in to put a face to 'the run away', and checked I was alright. 'Of course I'm not alright. You stupid people have ruined my plan and locked me up until I get fat!' Kelly was in the room too, leaning against the wall. She sat on my bed once the officer had left and looked at me disappointedly.

"Why did you do it Amy?" I hung my head and stared at the floor. I shrugged.

"Did you think it was clever?" She persisted.

"No, I've just had a bloody 'nough." I muttered from behind clenched teeth.

"Well it didn't get you anywhere did it? It's just proven to us how afraid of food you really are." I hadn't thought about that. Then again, I wasn't planning on being found out.

"I'm disappointed." She let me know, and left my room.

Throwing myself down on my bed, the air mattress gave an exhausted wheeze as it inflated, circulating more air to each crinkly corner of the substitute for a 'so called' bed... more like the deck of a tiny life boat, queasily bobbing over the ripples of troubled water. Everything; my whole life just seemed like a battle. A battle against good and evil, except, I didn't know which side was which. I couldn't differentiate between what I needed, and what I was thinking. It was a daze, a mist, a thick fog too dense for a knife's blade. Worries about my family penetrated my mind. What would they say? How did they view the situation? Was I ever going to get out of there? My head ached just thinking about it. And, to top it all off, Fay entered and sat beside me on my bed with bad news.

"Because you're so vulnerable at the moment Amy, and very low, we need to consider your safety..." She began, and I knew what was coming... "We're putting you on a one to one for a few days." Yep, I guessed it. Bloody brilliant! I burst into tears. This meant no being able to sneak food back to the toilet, no secret exercising, and no discussing plans with the others. So, all in all, the plan that had initially started out to help me lose weight ended up giving me a first class ticket to fat fighters! And so it was, Kelly started to follow me like a lost sheep, noting my occupation and whereabouts every ten minutes. I liked to get up and saunter to a different place every few seconds just to serve her right for invading my space. But, after figuring out she was not about to go anywhere, I gave up and retreated to a sofa in the corner of the lounge with a sketch book.

Art acted as an escape route for me. I could sit in one place for hours just sinking into a painting; enjoying the colours and feel of the brush and forgetting my problems. The tones seemed much more vibrant when I was in one of my depressive moods. I could 'get into' the feel of a picture when I was angry, and all my emotions poured out onto the page, creating an image bursting with energy. When my confidence and self belief were running low, my art pepped me back up again. It was something to be proud of and made me feel like a worthy person. I had a purpose when I drew, which gave me a reason to live for.

Art therapy was the next group to attend and I was ready to express my anger on the page. The picture I turned out contrasted drastically against the one I'd created in my second class. I chucked a load of random colours onto sugar paper and stabbed at it with a brush, whereas my first painting was of a tree trunk with printed bright hands for leaves and a sparkly rainbow above. This symbolised my happy childhood I frequently re-visited in my dreams. I found the thought of growing up difficult though. I held onto past memories that I treasured, which made me want to keep things the way they were- food, weight and all. These sessions also gave me the opportunity to have fun without the stress of being judged. I wasn't in college so I could paint as messily as I liked and still enjoy the experience. Having the chance to finger paint, hand print and use glitter reminded me of how I used to feel when I was small; painting in school and at the kitchen table, without a care in the world. I loved it and used every minute to forget and relax.

Max on the other hand was not interested one little bit. He slouched in his chair, twiddling a piece of pipe cleaner between his fingers, refusing to take part. He was rebelling against everything- education, walks, visits, even seeing his parents that travelled from Sheffield all the way to Altrincham just to be told that their son would not see them. I wondered how he could have been so shallow. Was he not human? Didn't he have feelings? Then again, I did sympathise with him from time to time. Being forced to face people, even your own family, at times when all you need is peace and company from your own breathing, is very aggravating and emotionally testing; especially when you are constantly worrying that everyone around you is out to judge you for your size.

Max was not the only one who was resenting 'the programme'. I had also had enough. Now that my plan had failed, eating food was an absolute crime to me. Even the thought of chewing and swallowing calories that would slither their way to my thighs was unbearable. I changed to Fortisip. This was a real step back for me, and would probably prolong my discharge. But I didn't care anymore. My whole life just seemed to revolve around how to escape food and the hospital, and I was sick to the back teeth of it. I was frightened of the drinks though; I didn't know what was in them. I was also weary whether they'd make me gain more weight quicker. Whatever the answer, I was certain they'd be easier to face than food.

"Actually they're not." Sharon had me know. "They bloat you like hell!" I didn't really care though, nothing could have been worse than cramming all that food in my mouth.

And so the next meal came and I was told to pick a flavour. Everyone recommended vanilla to me, so I took their word for it. A huge goblet of thick, sludgy, creamy liquid came in on a tray; a straw plunged into it. I took hold and stirred it round, squirming at the smell. After ten minutes I took a tiny sip and I knew from the first touch on the tongue it was impossible for me to drink that hideous calorie filled supplement. They offered to change the flavour as it was my first time, so I chose banana instead, which turned out to be just about bearable. However, when they returned with it, I'm sure they'd put more in than last time.

"There's more there than last time." I noted.

"No there isn't Amy", Abby replied. "I measured it accurately." In no mood to answer back, I made a reluctant start. Max on the other hand, who still hadn't touched his straw, lowered his head to the level of the table and peered at his drink in front of him, studying it in every dimension.

"I ain't havin mine, it's way more than I'm supposed to have."

"No Max", Abby reassured in an annoyed tone, "I measured yours as well and Kelly watched me do it."

"But it's not." He continued. And after a long dispute about a few millimetres of liquid, Kelly stormed back to the kitchen with his drink to be re-measured. She re entered.

"You were right Max." She accepted, "it wasn't the correct amount." Max grinned and sat back in his seat feeling rather proud with himself.

"Yeah, you were 3 centimetres short!" Everyone burst out laughing, apart from Max who slammed his head to the table in embarrassment! 'Better him than me' I thought.

After six different flavours, I finally found one that wasn't that bad: strawberry. So I'd make sure every night before I went to bed that the fridge had some in! The only down side to the drinks was that it was impossible to secrete parts of them into pockets or boots, which meant the whole calorie consumption had to be swallowed. Although, I have to hand it to myself, I did give it a pretty good shot... I remember one night when Rondo, (a night shift nurse), was on duty. He couldn't talk much English and, quite frankly, seemed in a world of his own most of the time. I took this to my advantage. He prepared the supper and took it down to the dining room on a tray; everyone behind him. I made sure to sit at the far end of the table so I had chance to carry out my plan. Once he'd handed me the goblet of calories, and was busy handing out everyone else's, I swiped a container with glitter at the bottom from the art cabinet behind me and poured my drink into it under the table. I glared into the pot which was now filled to the brim with swirly pink, sparkly liquid and placed it on the seat next to me. Quickly I stuck the straw from the empty cup into my mouth and made a slurping sound to hint I'd finished.

"Where'd drink go?" Rondo asked, looking me straight in the eyes.

"It all gone!" I gimmicked. A few giggles were exchanged, and I thought I'd gotten away with it, but Ellie, Emily and Max were peeping under the table to see what I'd done which gave the game away. Rondo called Rainie, the senior nurse on that night, from the office. She came in and saw the container of fortisip I'd discarded.

"Why d'ya do thart?" She looked at me crossly; her hands on her hips.

"Cos I didn't wan' it, and I ain't drinkin it!" I exclaimed in a defiant manner with my arms crossed tightly. Yet again, I was sent to my room. But I didn't care; as long as I didn't have to drink it, I wasn't bothered.

I remained on my 1:1 for a week. A whole bloody week being followed! I wasn't even allowed to go to the toilet without a member of staff watching me! And not to mention showers! There was one particular nurse though that really knew me and was ever so sympathetic towards my situation. She was Megan, and considerately sat on my bed round the corner whilst I had a shower. She trusted me. I'd met her on my first night on the ward. She was on duty with another kind, motherly woman called Belle. Megan's hair was so cool. It was short and red and spiky, and she had cool piercings in her ears. She was like the young grandma figure of the staff. She used to sit with me at night in my room and comfort me when I was down, and she was such a good hugger! Her deep, roughened voice reminded me of Deidre Barlow's off 'Corrie', and her sweet aroma made me feel safe!

When I'd finally been freed from my 1:1, which was agreed in ward round, I was so relieved. But I was soon to be aggravated again. My ward round wishes were to 'be freed, to get home leave for my great grandad's 85th birthday, and, (like I always added, in case there was the slightest chance of an agreement), to be discharged'! So yeah, I got freed, but that soon counted for nothing when I was told I didn't deserve to go home to my grandad's party. This sent me ballistic; it just through me and I snapped. After a good rant between me and my pillow, I marched down to Ellie's room.

"Would you mind if I waste some of your hair mousse Ellie?"

"No, no, not at all, use as much as you want." She answered, with a slight smirk on her face as if she knew what I was about to do.

"Cheers mate!" I patted her on the back and approached the hall wall with the bottle pointed in front of me. Eliza, who was a witness further down the hall saw me, and I glared cheekily into her eyes before pressing the head down, releasing a thick, white line of mousse across the wall! I dragged it the length of the corridor, spraying the pillar at the end.

"Stop it Amy." Eliza tried, but I was having none of it. I turned a corner and carried on straight down to the community room. I then gathered five rolls of toilet tissue and unravelled them through the hall ways, round my room and out the window, which wrapped itself in the wind around the magnolia tree outside! The adrenaline that was pumping through my veins was exhilarating. It felt so good to let my anger out. My heart had never beaten so hard and I shook from head to toe as I tried to take in my handy work!

My bedroom door swung open. "*What* do you think you are doing young lady?" Boomed Moira, turning red at the mere state of the ward.

"I'm sick of it, I'm sick of everything!" I yelled back. "They won't let me go home, it's not fair and I don't know what else they want from me!"

"Well I don't care whether it's fair or not. That does *not* give you the right to vandalise the ward!"

"Well I don't care either!" Was my reply. Moira approached me like an angry school teacher, thrusting the air with her finger.

"You will tidy this up *right* now. Go on. I'll watch you!" I couldn't believe it. She was actually making me clean up the entire mess by myself! I huffed as I snatched the paper from the floor and around the furniture. I was so embarrassed but proud of my defiance at the same time, as all the other patients from the ward were admiring my 'artistic' skills! No one else dared to do anything like that, especially when Moira, one of the strictest nurses on the ward, was on duty. She handed me a bucket filled with soapy water and a soppy cloth and watched as I scrubbed the walls clean. A smirk was pasted on my face during the entire punishment, to the other's amusement. And as if that wasn't enough, she marched into my room with a large plastic crate.

"You will put everything you can vandalise with in this box. You're not to be trusted with them." Now she had the cheek! She thrust my precious paints, pens, pencils, my shampoo, shower gel, hand wash, toothpaste and anything else that could make a mark, into the box and locked it away in the cupboard. The others couldn't believe Moira had confiscated *everything,* apart from the kitchen sink! At the same time as I was proud of my continuous defiance against 'the programme', I was really unnerved about having my shampoo taken from me. This was an essential item that I *really* did need. Every morning I washed my fringe and it was a rule for me to have it washed before anyone saw me. Now I had to leave my room with scruffy bed hair and a swollen red face just to ask for it. God I hated Moira. She had no right. I felt like swiping her glasses so she couldn't see! Ha! Now, that'd be funny!

Having nothing to do except read or play my psp on my bed, I used that time to think. And, glancing round at the treasured family photos from the previous year's summer holiday to Disney World Florida, the emotional pains of my, now under control, illness 'chilblain lupus' came flooding back. For months prior to going on that holiday of a life time, my illness hit an all time high and depression set in. The temperatures in my face would become sky high at spontaneous moments; I'd have no warning. The heat that spread across my cheeks and onto my ears and chin was unbearable. It wasn't just hot; the pain that came with it tightened my skin until each cheek felt like a freshly tuned drum skin. The psychological implications that came with it were equally as disturbing: I'd look as though I'd been smacked across my face, my nose was like Rudolf's and my eyes became dark, shadowy holes that lost their sparkle. To keep me cool I had to carry five or six freezing cold bottles of water around with me in a bag, plus an ice pack. Whenever I felt the pain coming I'd immediately feel the over whelming urge to thrust a cold pressure onto my face. It wasn't as simple as it sounds though; it was so embarrassing. I'd be sat in a café or a posh restaurant with my family, holding a huge icepack on one cheek and a bottle on the other. I felt the glare of a thousand eyes from every corner of the room, and a few sniggers and whispery comments, "Look at that girl over there...Weird!" It made me house bound. I didn't go out. I wouldn't. The fact that I had no clue as to when these spouts of flushes and pains would come meant I could never be sure I'd ruin the day out for me or my family by embarrassing us all.

The worst thing was that even when I was freezing, down to the minute details of tiny goose bumps lining my arms and back, these flushes still happened, so instead of wrapping up warm in the cold, I'd make myself even colder and in turn, more and more ill.

The doctors told me that applying cold surfaces directly to my face would scar me for life. I'd end up with a deep purple-blue vain-ridden rash across each cheek like sufferers from 'deep vein thrombosis' had. I didn't want that, but I *needed* those bottles. I started to wrap towels around the icepack to take the edge off the coldness and I'd cut down with the bottles, but still the flushes remained persistent and intent on ruining my life. I had to struggle through my GCSEs sat at my desk, which had no room for the paper, as it was taken up with bottles of ice. Stress made my flushes more frequent and even more painful, so the time of my GCSEs was a very low time for me. An idiot in my English exam, who was sat a few rows in front of me, turned around and asked in a peevish tone, "God, how many bloody bottles do you need?!" I felt like crying, he didn't understand, but it kept me determined; I wouldn't be beaten. I was a fighter, and still am.

Another experience that was supposed to be a good one was the end of school prom. It was a time when all the girls were busy glamour shopping for the best dresses in the shop windows, and cowered over magazines bursting with shimmering accessories. Everyone was excited about dressing up and slapping the makeup on. But I was the only one that was dreading it. Me and my mum had spotted the prettiest, most elegant prom dress we'd ever seen in a shop window months before the prom. I had to have it. We went in and tried it on and it looked great, but I stood there, staring at my reflection and for a moment, just a moment, I saw the girl that everybody else could see: the painfully thin, ill looking girl. My eyes swelled up and I remember saying to my mum through gushes of tears, "Mummy, I look so ugly; I'm too thin." I soon took this back though, when I started to resent my food again.

The day of the prom came and my mum had booked me in at the hairdressers. I hated the hairdressers. I abandoned such places and vowed never to step in one again after the last abominable cut, (which I won't give you the displeasure of going into). Anyway, I sat there fighting off the heat, with a noisy hand held fan, which was glowing inside my cheeks trying to fight its way up to the surface. I never had my hair in a different style, as this made me look different and I didn't like change. All I could do was wish the evening away so I could wash it out and stay indoors the following day. That night my mum applied my makeup and just as I was feeling like a proper young teenager, I could feel the prickly heat creep onto my cheeks and around the outsides of my ears. I couldn't fight it anymore and I knew the evening was over before it had begun. But to my astonishment, the foundation was so thick you couldn't tell I was bright red and rash-ridden underneath. The night turned out okay after all, but with a lot of initial stress.

The photo memories from Disney world Florida weren't just special to me because I absolutely loved Disney; it was because that was the turning point to the recovery of the painful hot flushes, and the good riddance to the unwanted bottles and ice packs. As much as I'd been looking forward to this wonderful holiday that'd we'd never forget, I was dreading it as well. What if I'd ruin the whole experience for myself and my family? What if the hot climate over there aggravated my flushes even more? What if they'd never leave me alone? So, what was supposed to be a relaxing and care free experience, (imagining the fun we'd have on holiday), brought about more stress.

During the plane ride there, I asked my dad to enquire for a bucket of ice to be placed under my chair in case I flared up on the journey. I was also wearing a strappy summer top and had all the air con vents turned on full and pointed in my direction, (minding not to blow my hair around though)! When we first got there, the heat hit me like a ton of bricks and I started to panic, but as I got used to it, I didn't flare up once during the whole holiday and I was absolutely astounded. I remember jumping for sheer joy around the villa we'd hired for a fortnight, punching and swooping the air with my fists. No one could explain it. Why had such hot temperatures treated me so kindly? What had changed? It didn't make any sense, but to be honest, I really didn't care as long as it never happened again. Of course, I was still stressing about if it would come back once I returned to cold Britain. But it didn't... hardly ever, anyway.

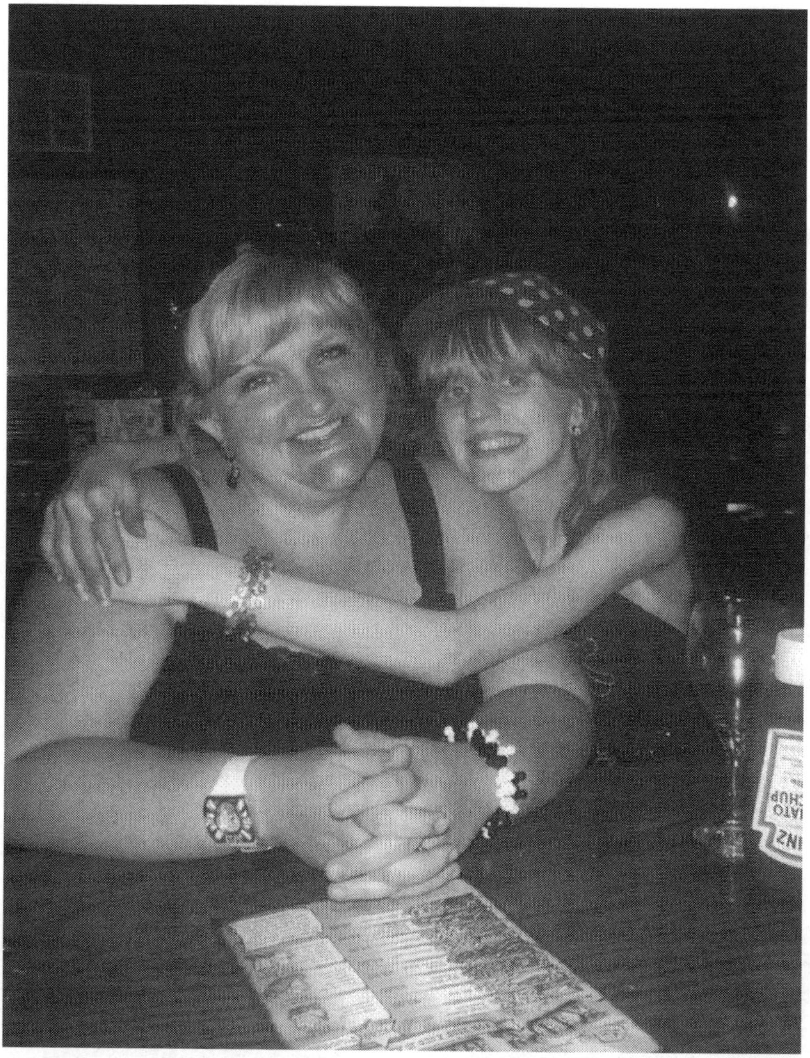

Just thinking back whilst sat on my hospital bed, I suddenly wished something upon myself that I'd never thought I'd witness myself think: I wished that I was a free girl again in the space of my own home; back in the days when my hot flushes ruled my life, instead of being a prisoner gaining weight in the hospital without the painful burden. That just proved how strongly I felt about not gaining the weight. I wouldn't wish what I'd gone through on anybody. Not even the biggest bullies and most evil murderers in the world. I had to question myself as to whether I'd actually just thought that or not. The flushes came a close second to the worst thing that had ever happened to me in my life, but the psychological anguish that tore through me from gaining weight un-doubtfully won every time.

If matters weren't tough enough, yet another new patient was to be admitted the following day. Her name was Charlie, a tall, thin girl with straight blonde hair and braces. I got the shivers when she came to look round the ward with nurses from general hospital that accompanied her. I walked out of my room and Fay, Charlie's tour guide, introduced me and I just wanted to shrink away. I bet Charlie was thinking, 'what the hell is she doing in an eating disorders unit? She's way too fat!' I slid round the corner into the lounge area where everyone else was hiding and pulled the sliding doors to.
"Aw, this is fuckin' awful!" Max moaned. "I hate this."
"Yeah, it's hard when a new patient comes," I admitted, "She looks alright though."
"No she doesn't." Sharon added, "She's from general, which means she has no idea how tough it is in private, and what's more she's dead thin cos I bet she's been gettin' away with murder!"
"Not anymore though", I sniggered, feeling a little reassurance that she'd definitely get no thinner whilst in the same care as us.
The next morning whilst in education, Charlie was admitted to the ward and eventually, come tea time, joined us at the

table. A plate of food sat before her and she grabbed the knife and fork and ate as though she hadn't eaten in ages. 'Wow, that was unexpected,' I thought with raised eyebrows, 'ah, there's still pudding yet, she'll never manage it!' But to my great surprise, she ordered the scariest thing on the whole menu…'Death by chocolate' cake.

"My favourite!" She exclaimed, and dug in! No- way- on- this- earth! I peered up at Megan from my straw full of Fortisip and gestured with my eyes a look of astonishment. She did the same. What was she doing on an eating disorders ward? She was obviously capable of eating normally. I was puzzled but suspicious at the same time: these doctors know, or, I'll rephrase that… *think* they know what they are doing, so if she hadn't an eating disorder, what were they thinking? I felt really sorry for her having to go through this unnecessary upsetting process for no reason whatsoever. Poor Charlie.

After tea I rang my mum and told her all about the strange new patient and what I'd witnessed. She couldn't believe it either, but reassured me the doctors knew what they were doing…hmm! The others were in disbelief too; they took the mick out of the events that happened at tea and we laughed at the doctor's silly misplacement.

"But why's she so thin?" asked Emily under a whisper, as not to catch earshot from the staff.

"That's exactly what I want to know." I answered. Charlie was put on bed rest because of her low weight and was only allowed out at night if she remained seated, which she hated. Emily had this problem, if we were all watching a film or sat in the lounge area, she'd refuse to sit down. This was to burn off extra energy standing up. I didn't really see the point in this as it hardly made any difference, but I understood that anything possible to burn off extra calories was a must. When the coast was clear of ear-wigging staff, I sat next to Charlie.

"Why are you here?" I asked. She shrugged. "Do you have an eating disorder?"

"No, I don't think so." She answered. Right, there was only one answer now, the doctors had definitely made a huge mistake and had obviously admitted the wrong girl. "Doctors seem to think I have anorexia cos I'm thin, but I haven't."

"Do you always eat chocolate n' stuff?" Emily asked, leaning further through the lounge alcove.

"Yeah, I eat normal, like I always have."

"And MacDonald's?" I was itching to know.

"Yeah."

Wow, this was not right. Why was she there? That was the golden question.

Over the next few days, like usual, Charlie would order cakes and ice creams from the menu, causing the rest of us patients to exchange looks of surprise and giggles down the table. The staff did seem impressed, but didn't react as surprised as I thought they would. However a couple of weeks into her admission, signs of stress and anguish were beginning to show. She'd sit for longer periods before touching her meals, she'd grow a pained look on her face as she took a fork full and eventually stopped ordering calorie-laden desserts. 'How could she have been finding the treatment hard if she was a normal kid?' I thought. But was she really a normal kid? Whenever we confronted her about it she stuck to her story about having no problem with eating, and told us she liked eating chips and donuts and allsorts of things. Everyone seemed convinced, apart from me. What she was saying just didn't add up. If she liked eating all of these, then she wouldn't show obvious signs of struggling. At first we all thought she was copying us, but eventually she cracked. Ever since she came out of weigh-in in her second week, she spoke to no one and even refused to eat certain meals. And after a diet increase, she lost it.

"AAaaaaah, I can't do this anymore, I'm fat!" We heard her shout at the dietician from her room. Then it died out in dribs and drabs of crying and sniffles.

"So she really has got an eating disorder!" Emily muttered under her breath.

"Yeah, I thought she might have." I replied. The clever devil; she had us all fooled, even me! Why hadn't I thought of that? Her plan was to pretend she could eat normally without stress for a period of time, which would cause the nurses to discharge her quickly, so then she could go back home and carry on getting thinner. She must have had will-power to do that though. To make yourself eat what you're terribly afraid of, in the chance that would prove you were normal in the long run, takes a lot. Yeah, maybe you'd put on a few pounds during the month of pretending to eat normally, but that plan would spare you kilo after kilo from your thighs when you end up being discharged months before you should.

So from then on she was a different person. She'd refuse to sit down, even on bed rest, she wouldn't come to education and she started to pick up on our little tricks to hide food.

"Have you always been on drinks?" she asked me.

"No, my diet plan is just so bloody huge at the moment I can't manage to eat all of it in solids." I replied, "But you don't want to be on them," I added, "They bloat you like mad and there's more fat in them." I didn't want Charlie to start drinks, because that would mean she seemed as ill as me, and my anorexia wouldn't allow that.

A week later, I'd earned a day home. I would have been allowed a whole weekend if I was on solids, but the rules say that if you're just on drinks then the most you can have is day-leave. Ah well, a day was better than none. The nurses gathered a few strawberry Fortisips from the fridge and put them in a bag for me to take home. Before I went though, they felt the need to show my dad my diet plan, as if they didn't trust me to do it myself...okay, okay, good point, they were wise not to trust me, but that's not what I wanted!

When I got home I ran to greet my mum and my sister and raced up the stairs to where my brother was 24/7: at his computer and Xbox, and gave them all huge, huge hugs. I shoved the Fortisip into the fridge and hid the diet plan in my pocket. My guinea pigs were still squeaking happily in their hutches outside and I loved to pick them up for a cuddle. I spent the day drawing at the kitchen table and chatting like I used to with my mum. I did my hair a couple of times, but tried my very, very best not to take up too much valuable free time. Even though I enjoyed being home, I avoided going outside in case someone noticed how fat I'd grown since they last saw me, so I kind of felt like a prisoner in my own home.

I remember when I first came to the ward and Lizzie told me that it becomes strange to go home after living in the ward for such a prolonged period. I thought that was absolute poppy cock, but now I was beginning to realise some truth in what she said. Being home didn't feel like home anymore; the hospital did. It felt like going to a friend's house and even the homely smell became strange to me.

Tea time came and I felt really awkward sat at the table with a huge glass of liquid, whilst everyone else had my mum's roast dinner. I liked my mum's cooking and secretly wished I'd had that rather than Fortisip, but a voice inside me wouldn't let me be 'normal', *"Avoiding solids lets people know how ill you are Amy. Now you're losing your thinness this is the only thing left to show you're ill; keep at it girl!."* I was kind of embarrassed actually: reaching for my straw every few seconds; taking measly sips then flicking it to the other side of the glass. At least being at home meant I could leave some Fortisip lingering at the bottom of the bottle, and didn't have to slurp every last droplet up like a vacuum cleaner on over-drive!

Back on the ward the mornings came and went and I became more and more frustrated. After waking up I'd look as though someone had greased my hair to my head and smacked me round the cheeks. I hated looking like this, especially as I still had to ask for my shampoo to be unlocked from the cupboard! And because I was aware of other people knowing what I looked like before I got myself feeling 'right', my anxiety levels were raised so high I was over flowing with paranoia. Perching myself on my desk; peering into the fun house mirror, (which I was convinced sniggered at my daft habits), whilst struggling with thin strands of hair, the room became wobbly. It was like being submerged into a never ending and confusing mirage with no real answer waiting for me. Michael had popped his head round the door numerous times during the 'obs' (observations), and told me to stand on the floor rather than sit on my desk, but sitting provided a much better view. So I stood, then when he shut the door I hopped straight back onto the table again! He wasn't thick though and he soon cottoned on. He brought a really high chair into my room. "Right, you sit on that. We don't want any broken bones if you fall from that desk!" Honestly, I felt like a right div!

That night I'd noticed another rough, red patch appear on my body; this time on my bum! It was really irritating so I decided to check it out. Geri was the nurse on that night. I liked her, even though she was the one who put me on this life destroying section! She came into my room whilst I was all tucked up and reading in the dim red glow from my side lamp. She kneeled down and had a chat with me and explained that it's really important to look after pressure marks to make sure they don't get infected. She needed to see it, and you know what that meant don't you? I reluctantly pulled down my pyjama shorts and shame set in. I didn't want her to see how fat I was underneath. The cure was simple: medicated cream and lots of checks, uuurrggh! However, there was a catch; an ugly one. I had to have an air cushion. So now I didn't just have to put up with a wheezy, bronchiectic bed, I had a groaning cushion n' all! They could have at least made it fashionable! It was bright blue and required a huge, bleeping battery pack attached to a thick black wire that needed plugging in.

At meal times it was a right burden. Everyone else would walk into the dining room, like normal people, and then there was me: heaving a lilo- like thing around whilst clumsily tripping over the wire. It made funny noises, just like the bed and I seemed to float up and down as the air pumped round inside it. I was now tall at the table, due to about five centimetres of air below me, and so found it harder to hide things.

I was even banned from sitting on the floor drawing in the lounge unless two cushions, minimum, were under me. I pretended to forget and only got away with it twice. Every other time the staff, particularly sharp eyed Amanda, would march me straight back to my room to fetch it! It was a symbol of how thin I must have been to have needed it, but knew it was only there to help me. It was so degrading.

However degrading that might have been, nothing compared to having problems wetting the bed. I'd always had a problem with that, ever since I was a little girl. I knew it had something to do with stress and being unsettled, but there must have been more to it than that because it was just getting out of hand. I couldn't hold it for long and I'd unconsciously wet the seat I was sat on if I fell asleep. The nurses knew about my problem and it was really difficult to keep it discreet from the other patients. Kelly did a one-off week of night shifts and I was so humiliated when I woke up in the middle of the night lying in a round, soggy patch! I didn't want her to know about it, so I ran into my bathroom and lay lots of towels on my mattress, then quickly cleaned myself up and dived back under the covers in the nick of time. The next morning I told Megan about it. I felt comfortable telling her because she was much older than I was and had probably dealt with this sort of thing before. She was great about it, but when we came back from education; my bedroom door was wide open, baring its inners for the world to see, including my mattress which was turned on one side against the wall. Everyone asked why that was and I came up with this pathetic excuse that, "a spring popped through the mattress and was poking me, so needed replacing!" Yeah right! That's what everyone thought I bet. They could probably guess what it was but I was far too embarrassed to admit to it; I was the eldest there for god sake!

    During one of these stressful episodes is where one group in particular came in handy: 'Relaxation' or 'Chill with El', as it was later to be re-named. I loved this group and I remember my very first session I went to. Eliza would dim the lights in the bean-bag or community room whilst we'd sink ourselves into giant black leather beanbags. Soft music of running water and birdsong would fill the room, and El would begin to read out soothing passages in a quiet voice. Her words made every muscle in our bodies relax; right from our heads down to our toes. She always sent me into a deep sleep that she had to shake me out of! Apart from bedtime, it was one of the only times I had to completely shut off from the maddening world that was growing rapidly around me. Weird, distorted images of bright colours and patterns used to imprint themselves on the corneas of my eyes, and the vivid, ghostly shadow they left were still there when I woke. Do you know that lazy feeling you get when you wake up in the morning and the weight of the world seems to have drifted off into a forgotten place in the night? Well, that's what 'Relaxation' made you feel: groggy, but content at the same time; and as though nothing mattered anymore except you. It was a good place, a relaxing place and a place where we also had fun. I remember one session where Sharon went totally under, and she was snoring and everything! It was so funny.

'Relaxation' group would have been really appropriate on the spontaneous day of 'room search'. Early one morning, the staff decided to do a random search of everyone's room to check no hiding of food or traces of sick or self-harming objects or anything like that was being hidden, and I had a gut feeling that they'd discover my rocks in my draw and cotton onto my 'weight meddling'. I was trying to reassure myself all morning that I'd completely disposed of any crumbs and crusts and anything, but I couldn't think of one thing I hadn't hidden properly.

The day dragged on, like usual, and no one had found anything suspicious, (or so I thought). We all headed down to the ward after education, and on entering, Amanda was stood outside my door with her hands placed firmly on her hips; a glare in her eye. She did the finger gesture as if to say 'come here'! The others parted and I followed her into my room with my head turned to the floor.

"Right young lady, why do you think I'm disappointed with you?" She asked in a low toned voice, looking down at me with folded arms. My heart started to beat vigorously and I began to fiddle with the ends of my hair. A thousand reasons sprung to mind: crumbs on the floor maybe; some crust that had missed the toilet; bits of biscuit in my shoes, but I didn't want to say, just in case it was something else. An awkward silence lingered.

"I'll give you a clue shall I?" She wrenched open the bathroom door and grabbed my bright pink fluffy dressing gown, and, reaching into its pockets, "Albran!" she pulled the dried sticks out and pushed them under my nose.

"How did they get there?" I asked through a giggle.

"You know full well, and wipe that smirk off your face. This will not be forgotten. I'll have to report this back to the other nurses." She left and I just dug my head into a pillow and screamed at it! That albran must have been there for weeks. I must have hidden it there when I was making my own breakfast!

After eight long, agonising weeks since I'd been placed on my section and of phone calls and visits from my advocate, Barbra and my chosen solicitor, had passed, the day of the tribunal was finally, finally here. I was one hundred percent convinced I was going to get discharged. Everything was on my side: I had consumed all my meals for the past few weeks; I'd eaten fine on my supervised meal; I'd been eating/drinking without fuss whilst on home leave, and this was all whilst battling the physical and emotional pain of gaining weight. What had I to lose?

Megan led me to the dining room for what I believed would be my last snack as a patient at the hospital. I'd even chosen to eat it in solid food, just to impress the tribunal. Sharon even gave me her toffee flavoured yogurt she was saving and wished me all the best. The night before, she and I had sauntered up to the beanbag room and lit all the colourful bubble tanks to pray for our 'freedom'. We knelt on the big sacks with our hands together; almost in tears pleading God to let us out.

After my snack I retreated to my room where my mum and dad had arrived and were waiting for me. A brand new Minnie mouse t-shirt was laid on my bed, my mum stood crying beside it.

"I don't think I can do this anymore Amy." My mum sobbed into my shoulder. "I just want everything to be normal." I squeezed my mum tight and looked her straight into her watery, deep blue eyes, "Don't worry mummy, everything will be fine and I'll be home again with you and daddy and Daniel and Brooke, and we'll all be happy." She cried harder, so I wiped her warm tears with my finger tips and kissed her cheek. My dad was stood in the corner of the room, obviously trying to block out the 'nonsense' pouring out of my mouth. I didn't want to look at him. I had nothing to say. If he didn't want to back me up and help do what was right for me, I didn't want anything to do with him. Just as things were getting emotional, Dr.Waissel knocked and entered the room. She looked confident, but doubtful too; so she should have been n'all! I had everything going for me and I deserved to speak up for myself, and that was exactly what I was about to do. On exiting my room though, I quickly ran over to the coffee table in the lounge where the others were waiting to see me off. I opened Sharon's palm and slipped some paperclips inside, "These are lucky paper clips. As long as you have your paperclips, everything will be alright." I whispered into her ear, closing her palm tight. Everyone wished me luck and I exited the ward.

    The tribunal was to be held at The Grange in a very formal meeting room. The tall mahogany door opened and a small, middle-aged woman, wearing half moon shaped spectacles, stood at its entry clasping the brass handle firmly. I spotted my advocate, Barbra, over the crowd of bobbing heads all piling into the tiny room, entering The Grange, along with my solicitor. A few friendly faces on my side were a pleasure to see. On entering I noticed three important looking figures seated, with equal distance between them, at a long table facing us. They each had a wod of paper in front of them, along with a red, a blue and a black pen each. They shuffled the sheets and adjusted their glasses before they begun. The middle woman spoke first, "Good morning. Welcome to Amy's", glancing at me over her specs, "tribunal. We are gathered to discuss the 'section three under the mental health act', which Amy accuses the hospital of wrongly placing her." I heard a cough, or rather; a clearance of the throat, and it came from my left. It was Dr.Waissel. I knew she just couldn't wait to open her 'experienced' gob to stick her claws deep into the one chance I had of getting out of there. I gave her a stare and re focused on the meeting, squeezing my mum's hand every second of the way.

    "Firstly, as it is Amy's tribunal, we shall begin her." She turned her head to me, "Amy, please explain to everyone how you feel about your current situation regarding your sectioning whilst under the care of the hospital." My heart rate doubled and the exasperating feeling of adrenalin pumped into every muscle in my body. I'd spent every night conjuring the exact words to say to them. This was my moment, and the only one I had to get it right. I had to do this. And I let them have it.

"Hiya everyone, as you know I'm Amy!" I tugged on the collar of my shirt, "I feel extremely wrongly done by, having being placed on this unnecessary section which I believe is hindering my recovery. As you have read in the reports about me, I have complied fully with the programme and have continued to eat what I'm told whilst at home with my parents, and I know I can do this without having the added pressure of a section looming over me. Being on the section makes me more nervous. It gives me less control of my situation, which is having a huge impact on my OCD. The only reason I came here was for the treatment of my OCD. That is what is causing me so much emotional pain. I wanted therapy, helping me to deal with the messages I'm getting in my head, and so far I've received none whatsoever; just had food forced into me, which has not helped one bit. And I know you all feel better for the section because that gives you all the control over me and what I do, but I want independence on this. I feel cheated to be honest."

The room fell silent, with only the odd cough and a shuffle breaking the atmosphere. There was so much more I wanted to say, but that summed it up at least.

I began to cry when my mum's turn came. I could tell this was the worst moment of her life. She desperately wanted me to get better, but at the same time, her duty as a loving mother told her to do what I wanted her to: say she wants me out. So she did.

"I think Amy is coping with the treatment very well. She is complying with her diet plan at home and I'm proud of her. I feel the section is unnecessary." She choked on her words as she said them, and was unable to look anyone in the eye except me. I clutched her hand tight and leant on her shoulder. 'Thanks mummy,' I thought, 'I love you so much.' After mine and my mum's views were out, I felt no one could top that. But then there was my dad.

"I feel the level of care being given here by the nurses and the doctors is outstanding, and believe they are doing Amy a world of good. I'd like her to stay and complete the treatment for her own health and well being." He said this as calm as a cucumber. My mum and I gave him a stare. Honestly, I could have strangled him! How could he have been so mean and self centred. He knew what we believed was best for me, but he blatantly ignored that and chose to follow his own ignorant head! I hated him more than ever and couldn't wait to lay into him once the meeting had finished.

    Just as I thought things couldn't look any worse for me, the tribunal only went and asked my Cahms worker his opinion, and we all knew what *that* was going to be. He basically stuttered in his mumbling way how I was 'supposedly' extremely ill and still very underweight, and that the section wasn't ready to be lifted yet. What a load of bollocks! I felt like shouting, 'Stop chatting shit and have a heart you frigging moron!' But that wouldn't have got me anywhere, so I kept it buttoned.

    As the meeting went on, things looked worse and worse for me, especially when it came to Waissel's turn, but I won't even go there! The room was split in two. There was my army: Me, my mum, Barbara and my solicitor. Then there was Waissel's army: Her, my dad, my Cahms worker, a ward nurse, and the Tribunal by the looks of things. After two hours of fighting for my freedom however, the hearing was finally over. That was it. There was nothing more I could do. They had to let me out. They just had to. There was no life for me at a heavier weight than I was. My mum and I walked back to the ward to wait for the verdict, which would be delivered by my solicitor and my dad. I was planning what I'd do when I got out with my mum. I'd run straight to the guinea pigs and give them all a big tickle and some treats. Then I'd draw some pictures and watch Disney films with my mum. I couldn't wait. But my dreams were abruptly shattered when the decision came back from the meeting. My dad looked down at me, and my solicitor didn't look happy. He shook his head.

    "I'm really sorry Amy. I tried my best, but the Tribunal have decided it is in your best interest to stay under the section for the time being." I was speechless. Even though I had been expecting this, I never actually thought how I'd react to it. My face shrivelled into weeping as my salty tears poured over my mum's shoulder. She began to cry too. She knew how miserable I was and worried I'd do something silly. That was the worst day of my life. It was as if a bottomless black hole was engulfing me; disabling my abilities to control what I did. The room looked spinney and my brain pounded against my skull. I hated everything and everyone at that moment. My world was over.

The other patients were really shocked I hadn't got out. They knew how hard I was trying and felt so sorry for me. Sharon threw away the apparently 'lucky paperclips' I gave her, as they had proven very bad luck for me. The following few days I was so quiet no one would have thought I was even there. They were like a cd on repeat, and were structured something like this: Get up, Breakfast, sit in room, Lunch, sit in room, tea, sit in room, supper, bed. The four blank walls of my square room caged me in like an animal. The harder I stared at the whiteness, the more I saw luminous pictures of strange characters appear on the corneas of my eyes before me. 'Wheeze, wheeze' went the mattress, 'scream, scream' yelled the tormented patients, 'FAT, FAT' went my head. All these things swirled into one murky, mixed-up potion of darkness and poisoned my mind with toxic thoughts of self-hate. I used to ram my fingers in my ears and bury my face deep down in my pillow and cry myself to sleep. Honestly, it was that bad. I know it probably seems like nothing to you- putting a bit of weight on, but for me, it was the end of the world. It just wasn't bearable to think about.

The one thing that seemed even remotely important now was my escape. Nothing had worked. If they weren't going to let me go even though I was eating without fuss, and if they weren't even listening to me, then this called for an escape so fool-proof, no one would even suspect the place I'd flee to. I couldn't escape from the ward again, as that was far too risky; plus they had their eyes sharpened as I'd done it before. This escape had to be done from home. I had to wait for home leave, and, considering the state I was in after the news that I hadn't been let out, the chances of home leave for at least a few weeks were looking slim. This meant me putting on yet another face in order to claim leave sooner rather than later.

Education soon became a breeding ground for my thoughts and plans to cultivate and develop. I suddenly lost interest in artistic activities, and I no longer participated in group activities. I needed a way to plan my escape route, and the only way to do that was via the internet. Li leant me her computer, as I said I was going to do some research for an art project at college. But of course, that was a load of bull! When she departed from the room, I opened up a 'taxis to Manchester airport' page and a map of the city. I needed to know how much money I was going to need for such a large journey too, so I checked the price lists. I was careful to minimise the page when Li popped in every minute or so, but eventually she caught sight of what I was looking at. I quickly deleted the page and said in a fluster, "Oh, Li, I'm just checking the taxi firms for my mate. She's going on holiday you see, and she needs to know where to get a taxi!" What a pathetic excuse! But it was on the spur of the moment.

On the way back to the ward, my sudden hot sweat cooled down with the gust of the wind, and my mind stopped worrying about what Li saw. However, my worries turned to reality when Sandra called me into my room with a concerned look on her face. She sat down on my bed; me on my chair, and talk about patronising! She made me feel tiny, (excuse the pun)!

"Now, Amy, can you tell me why you think I'm here?" Hmmm, let me think about that! I didn't know whether to lie through my teeth or to bluff my way out of it.

"It's bout what I was looking at on the computer at education isn't it? I know what it looks like, and I know what you're going to say, but that is just r-e-d-i-c-u-l-o-u-s!" I rambled out at high pace.

"What does it look like, Amy?" Sandra sarcastically asked with a smirk pasted across her mouth. Now I knew Li had rung over to the ward and ragged on what I was up to.

"It looks like I'm going to run away on a plane somewhere doesn't it?" I was quick to reiterate.

"Well that's certainly what we're concerned about. Do you see why we have to check this out? We wouldn't be doing our job if we didn't, and we want to keep you safe." She continued. 'Yeah bloody right', I thought, 'you just want to cover the skins on your own backs from us suing you!'

"Yes of course," I said through gritted teeth, "but you are seriously mistaken. I could NEVER do anything like that to my family; especially not after last time." At hearing myself say this, it was so hard to admit to myself that this was a lie. It was the hardest lie I've ever had to tell. Of course I couldn't dream of doing such a thing, but when someone's in a position like mine with a demon on your back, and a constant voice in your head, you'd do anything to escape the reality. I tried really hard to put on my most serious and genuine look. I stared her hard in the eyes and swore on my life, (with my fingers crossed obviously), that it wasn't what it seemed.

After a long interrogation, I realised getting a plane was not an option. Sandra had rang my parents and informed them of the events of the afternoon, and consequently told them to remove any form of ID and passport from my reach. Damn! I had the perfect plan. It was in my dad's top draw with the others. Now I had no idea where to look. So it seemed the farthest I could go was London or somewhere like that via train. And no, of course I had no idea how to go about catching a train, but I had a tongue in my head, so I'd use it!

I needed to share my secret plans with someone, just to get them off my chest and ask for advice. However, I had to be very careful who to confide in. Not everybody could be trusted. And as much as I wanted to tell Ellie, I just couldn't, because I knew Sharon would force it out of her. But I knew one person who I knew wouldn't utter a word to a fly. Emily.

That night I approached her in the hallway and began a discussion to do with escape and told her all my feelings about the place. She was totally all-for-me going. She confirmed my thoughts that nothing else had worked to get me out of there, so if extreme measures were needed to speak my feelings, so be it. I was relieved Emily shared the same views as me. And a bit of support was what I really needed. We exchanged mobile numbers, so when the time came we'd be able to update each other on people's whereabouts and just chitchat in general. She swore not to say anything, and we shook on it.

There was really no point in eating now if there was nothing to work towards, like a tribunal, to prove my point. But if I refused to cooperate, home leave wouldn't happen, and I'd be stuck on the ward to gain the pounds forever more. This thought pained me to think about. It was so unfair and such a one sided battle either way I looked at it: Either I had to eat and gain weight to leave permanently, or I still had to eat and gain some weight for me to escape! I couldn't flee from the reality. However, when I balanced both options up, the second out weighed the other considerably: yes I might gain some weight, but it would be no where near the amount I'd gain if I stayed for the full duration of my admission.

Every night, escape routes flooded my brain, and I encouraged myself to eat just for the chance of escape. I'd once had visions of a plane leaving the ground with me on it; not knowing where it was going; all my troubles left behind me. But now that was shattered. Thank god for trains!

The other side of my mind, which I resembled with an angel figure, never let it lie that I had so many people who loved me and so much going for me, and I knew this. But I just couldn't possibly be happy and successful when I'd be uncomfortable in my own skin. It was true though, I had lots of lovely people who supported me, including my next door neighbours, 'the Royale' family. I'd known them for years and they were really nice, friendly people. As soon as they'd heard about me going into hospital, they'd gotten a huge bouquet of flowers from their dad's florist shop for my hospital room, which they replaced regularly with a fresh set of colours. They came to visit a lot too, and I appreciated this so much as it was quite a distance to travel just for me. Whenever Sophie and Madeline Royale visited, I felt so happy and almost as if I wasn't going through that nightmare any longer. We'd chat about girly things and days out we could look forward to. They're truly some of the nicest people I've ever met and I love them to bits.

I had a surprise the next day. Abby was on duty and wrote on the board who had visits that day.

"No Abby," I interrupted, her flow of writing fading off, as I saw she'd written my name, "I don't have visitors today." She looked at me puzzled, and then down at the ring binder she held in her hand.

"Yes you do, Amy." She replied. That was weird. No one had told me of anyone visiting.

"Who's coming?" I asked, looking rather baffled. There was a pause as she read the name scrawled in the book...

"Jazmine Franks."

No way!

"Really?" I asked in a high pitched voice.

"Well that's what it says, yeah." Oh my god I couldn't believe it. Jazmine was a lovely girl I'd known throughout school. But I classed her as one of 'the popular' kids and never in a million years would have dreamt she'd want to come and visit me! I was so happy, and I felt privileged to have her visiting. I told everyone else on the ward and I felt a sense of importance all of a sudden.

When she came, later that afternoon, we had such a good chat. I don't think she knew exactly what was going on in my mind for me to have gotten so ill: no one would've, so I explained the best I could. She filled up and started to cry, and at that moment I realised just how much people do love me and want me to be happy and get better. I felt really bad, as this is an illness that logically, the person affected can help really, but it's not that simple. I comforted her and she just wanted me to be like I was again; healthy, so I could continue with my life. I gave her a huge hug and promised I would try. She'd heard about my last escape attempt, and even though we laughed at it, I could tell she was trying to stop herself from crying and told me never to do anything like that again. When she said this, I sort of thought twice about what I was planning to do, but I just had to do it. I reassured her as much as I could, but added, "I'll look after myself", as not to promise something I could not keep.

And so the days went on: Breakfast, snack, lunch, snack, tea, supper, bed etc, etc. I had to haul my way through each day; all of us did. But at least for me I still had that one driving force behind me. One day soon I'd get out of there, and return to my rightful size and life. I often wondered, whilst sat sketching in the lounge area, what it must have been like for the rest of the girls to have no aspiration or drive to even attempt escape. They knew for certain they were gaining weight everyday without their control. That must have been terrifying. This thought made me all the more for doing a runner. I had to. It wasn't an option not to try.

Meanwhile, although Max wasn't planning any escape attempts, he had his own little routine he'd carry out all day everyday to make him feel better about consuming things ED was telling him he should not. He'd slurp down each drink of fortisip in record speed so he had less time to wait before he could walk it off. As soon as he left the table, he'd walk straight to his room and continue to pace up and down, up and down until the next meal: Round his room, up the corridors, round the lounge, round the dining table, the community room. You name it; he'd walked a marathon round it! He refused to sit down unless it was at meal times, and he'd speed on walks. The staff weren't having it though. They banned him to his room. But that didn't stop him. He'd just walk round his room in circles all day! Eventually the staff started threatening him with room rest and chair rest, which meant he was not allowed to even get up, never mind walk, but I don't think this bothered him. He'd told himself he had to do this, and so he did. As his diet increased, he'd calculate how many more minutes he'd have to walk per day, but there simply weren't enough hours in a day. This is where night came in handy: he rarely slept, so I'm assuming he used this extra time, in between checks, to make up the pacing.

Amber was allowed more and more home leave and extra opportunities to leave the ward than everyone else, and for no apparent reason. We were really miffed about that. Apparently, according to Dr.Waissel, 'everyone's situation is different, and everyone's care plan isn't the same.' What a load of bollocks! Of course we were the same. At the end of the day, we all had an eating disorder, and were being given the same treatment in the same home, and so deserved to be treated equally.

"Did you know Amber might be getting discharged way under weight?" Sharon announced to the rest of us.

"No way!" I replied, "That's so unfair. Why does she deserve to be let go? Is it because she's the favourite? Is it because her parents are really good pals with Dr.Waissel? If so, that's not on. I ain't having it!" Sharon gave me a look of despair.

"No Amy, it's none of those reasons. It's because she is the only one who isn't on section 3 of the mental health act." I couldn't believe it. One piece of paper with some crap scrawled on it had the dominant power of deciding whether we could be freed or not! This was outrage.

"Lucky sod", added Ellie, "wish I was her." We nodded in agreement. We felt so wrong-done-by. Life was so unfair, and it felt like God hated us all.

Another painstakingly agonising week filled with snacks and calories and fat came and went, and I'd finally built up enough trust and gained enough weight to be allowed home that coming weekend. I was so excited. I'd been waiting for that day for what felt like a lifetime, and I was ready to put my plan into action. The shear thought of running away sent a thrill rushing through my bones, and I finally felt as if I had some power back over my life since ED was being forced out of me. Throughout the time that lead up to that opportunity of home leave, all I was thinking to myself whilst eating was, 'you suckers! You don't even have a clue what I'm planning to do, do you?! Call yourself professionals? Pfft, what evs!" I couldn't help but feel smug and overwhelmed with my 'genius'! Emily and I were the only ones who knew, and I was dying to tell Ellie. But I was so close I couldn't risk Sharon getting it out of her. I had to hold my tongue and carryout the plan before anyone was informed of my disappearance.

The morning of home leave came, and I made sure I had everything I would need packed up and ready to use: brushes, bobbles, clips, hairdryer, straighteners, sketch books, pencils, phone, stamps, letters, money; everything I could possibly need to survive out and about by myself. I remember saying goodbye to my friends. It was so hard. What if I never saw them again? They were the only people who properly understood my situation, and they had been the best friends I'd ever had. I didn't want to leave them. I wanted to support them as much as I needed them to support me. But I had to. I didn't have a choice. I told Ellie I'd see her later and squeezed her tight. Emily gave me a big hug too, and told me to be careful and that she was only at the other end of the phone if I needed her. My eyes filled up and I felt a tear trickle down my cheek. I couldn't express my emotions in front of the staff though. It would've given my plan away. I peered back into my hospital room filled with home comforts: my favourite teddy bears, my artwork, Barry's materials he'd left me, precious photographs, loving get well notes, gifts, college work, and I couldn't help feel my stomach turn. I couldn't bare leaving all my things behind; all I would ever need to pursue my future career in art and all my memories of my family and my 'thin' past life. But my feelings about weight and the way I was dominated over everything. I thought, 'as soon as I leave this room, my life is over. Everyone will hate me, and I'll have nothing to show for anything I've ever achieved.' It made me very sad to think like this, and in a way, I felt terrible for continuing with my plan. But I'd come so far, and it would be silly to stop there. I whispered a silent goodbye to my belongings and leant out of my room and into the ward corridor. 'DING-DONG!' my dad was here. I was ready to leave. One last secretive glance over to Emily, a nod of the head, and then I was gone.

Three days and two nights home leave is what I'd earned: Saturday till Monday. 'Should I go on the Saturday?' I asked myself, 'or would the Sunday be better..... or the Monday?' I couldn't decide when to go. I think I was just so panicky about the whole situation I didn't have a clue what I was thinking. It was a shock to me that I was still going through with it! How could I do that to my family? What on earth was I thinking? Well, that's the power of ED for you. I was determined to eat solid food whilst I was at home, as it had fewer calories in it. Plus, I could hide things much easier at home; you can't hide drinks!

On the Saturday morning, my mum and everyone were so pleased to have me back home, and so was I. It's just; I knew what I was about to do, and this made me very, very upset inside.

"I've bought you some salmon with herbs for your tea, and some special rice and salad." My mum announced, "Just what you like." Could the guilt have gotten any worse? I was grateful she'd put so much effort into my stay at home, but I really wished she hadn't bothered this time, as I knew I wouldn't be there to appreciate her hard work.

"Thank you Mummy." That's all I could think of to say. It was a fine June day, so my mum, dad and sister decided to pop out for the afternoon. Obviously I didn't want to go, for it was a perfect opportunity for me to disappear. My brother stayed at home too on his video games.

"I love you mummy", I said as I gave her a big hug, "Always remember that." She gave me a funny look.

You aren't going anywhere are you, Amy?" I paused. I looked her I the eye, and told the hardest lie I've ever had to in my life.

"I promise, why would I do that? I love you. See you later."

"Are you sure?" She asked. "You wouldn't go away would you?" The persistent questions made me want to confide in her, but I couldn't; my plan wouldn't work and I'd be back to the hospital for months.

"I promise."

After they'd left, I silently packed the relevant objects into a back pack and loaded up two A2 folders, bursting at the seams with watercolour paper, paints and brushes, and mixing plates. I couldn't leave my art things behind! My plan was to flee to London and set up my own little spot on the streets, where I'd paint scenery and portraits for money. I heaved the two folders and my back pack past my brother's room, where he was noisily playing on his Xbox, down the stairs and out through the front door. I leant them against the bench outside the porch and ran back inside.

"Daniel?" I shouted

"Yeah?"

"I'm just going to Jennifer's, I won't be too long."

"Okay" he replied, half listening.
"...I love you." I added, but he was far too busy to hear. The folders proved way too heavy to carry all that way; especially to lug around London. I had to leave them behind. I really didn't want to. It was my life in those folders, but to get away in time, and practically, there was no other way. I unlocked the door and ran back inside.

"Forgot my bag!" I shouted up to Dan; covering my tracks. I dragged them upstairs as quickly as I could and fled back down them, off the drive, up the street and to the bus stop. If things couldn't have gotten more awkward, a lady we were very friendly with, who lived above the post office approached the bus stop from the opposite direction. She asked where I was going. I was hesitant, but surprisingly confident in my reply.

"I'm going to my friend's house." She seemed to buy my alibi and swiftly passed.

However on the bus, the nerves were getting to me a little. I clutched the side bar so hard my knuckles appeared white, and my heart felt as though it was about to pound through my chest and plunge to the floor. I couldn't believe it. I was actually at stage one of my plan. And it had gone successfully so far. Even though that bus journey was very familiar to me, it seemed the longest, most confusing bus journey I'd ever taken. I stared out of the side window all the way; my mind wandering who I would bump into, how my family would react, and if I'd be safe. I could feel my eyes fill up with tears as my sight became murky behind the gathering water, and I swallowed hard. There was a huge stubborn knot in my throat that refused to budge. It was all the guilt mounting up into a ball.

When the bus finally arrived in Bury, I shakily stumbled off, tugging down the peak of my hat to hide my face, and clutching my backpack tight. Speed walking, I half sprinted down the flights of concrete steps to the met, shoved I don't know how many coins into the pay machine and ran onto the tram without collecting my change. With each stop that passed, the more guilt seemed to pour through the doors. My heart was still beating like a racehorse and I began to get fidgety. Every few seconds I felt the increasing need to slouch in my chair, tug on my hat and scan my eyes up and down the corridor, just in case anyone I knew happened to get on. They didn't, but I was on my guard. The journey was extra hard for me, as I was familiar with it, and reminded me of so many happy memories with friends and family where we'd used the met for transport. I had to ignore those feelings though. I just had to.

I was wearing a sleeveless summer top, thin grey trousers, converse shoes and a baker boy hat. I was still *just* on the 'thin' side for my liking, and liked to show off my thin arms to the strangers that passed by at Victoria station in Manchester. The warm summer breeze blew through the station, through my hair and pushed past my shoulders, slightly cooling the sweat that was beginning to crawl up my back. I raced to the board that lit up with all the destinations and times for train departures in alarming orange lights. My eyes scoured the board for 'London', but it wasn't there. My heart sank. I must have stood there for at least ten minutes completely baffled by the frequently changing boards ahead of me, when I noticed 'Leeds' lit up in the top left hand corner. Bingo! It departed at 5pm: in fifteen minute's time. But then came the hard part...actually *buying* the ticket! Never in my life had I bought a train ticket, and I needed to hurry before the train left me behind. I approached a tall looking, beefy blue machine, and letting people ahead of me in the queue, I observed them purchasing a ticket. But when it came to my turn, it was far too complicated. Too many coloured buttons and random words on the screen. I was getting frustrated with myself. 'How hard is it to buy a bleeding train ticket?'

I stepped back from the machines and a short; rough, yet friendly looking cleaning man caught my eye. He obviously worked there, as he wore a name badge and had a bin bag and a rubbish picking stick in his right hand.

"Erm, excuse me?"

"Yeah" He answered.

"Well, err; I was wandering, you see, how do you go about buying a train ticket?" He looked up to the right and scratched his head. And with a crinkled brow, he approached the machines. In all honesty, he looked as confused, if not more so, than I was.

"Uuurrggh" He grunted, and after a pause, "Follow me." He led me to a desk set back into a smart wooden section of a wall.

"Pay here." He said

"Thank you."

I had to stand on tippy toe to see the woman perched behind the counter. She was short and middle aged looking; very nice.

"Excuse me, is this where I pay for a train ticket?" My heart began to beat faster again. I was worrying how old you needed to be to buy a ticket. I hadn't thought about that part.

"Yes it is young lady. How may I help you?"

"Please could I buy a ticket for the next train out to Leeds?" I asked in my most confident and mature sounding voice.

"Of course. How old are you?" This is where I pondered for a bit. I knew child prices would be cheaper, but if I lied and said I was younger than I was, she might not have let me go when I was by myself. It wasn't worth risking.

"I'm sixteen." She looked at me in astonishment.

"No way? Really? You're sixteen?" She asked, her voice becoming higher in pitch as she went on.

"Err….yeah!" I raised my eyebrows slightly and gave her a grin.

"No offence, you look about twelve!" She called over to another work mate. "Hey Carol, Carol. Come here." Another woman, slightly taller with a bee-hive hair do, came over behind the counter. "This girl here. She's sixteen!" They both stood there gob smacked. I thought this was so funny it was unbelievable!

"I'm sorry love, I'm going to have to charge you adult price now. If you'd said you were 14 I'd have believed you, and I'd have charged you a kids price."

"Then can you just pretend I'm a child and forget I told you that?" I had the cheek to pluck up.

"No, sorry I can't do that now I know." Adult price was almost double child's: 37 bloody quid for an adult ticket! Scandal!

"One way or two?" She asked.

"One" (obviously). I wasn't planning on coming back until the doctors agreed to discharge me.

I found my train. It seemed deserted, but I knew it was the right one because of the huge lit up sign on the platform that read 'Leeds, 5pm train'. I noticed a door slightly ajar at the back of the train, so I slid through the gap and perched myself on a back seat. Keeping my head bowed under the brim of my hat, I felt the cooling breeze of passengers entering the train run up my arms. I hunched over and hugged my bag tight. I was alone. Pairs of legs passed down the corridor and took seats in the middle carriages. I was glad for the space. I didn't want to be seen alone, as this might have seemed suspicious. There was a fold-down table attached to the back of the seat in front, which I began to unpack the contents of my bag onto. My phone lay at the bottom: Sixteen miss calls. Six unread texts. My heart began to thump again. The realisation that I hadn't gone to Jennifer's had set in back home. I just stared hard at my phone; my hand quaking at all the decisions I had to make. I unlocked it and read them, one by one.

Mum. 'Where are you? I know you're not at Jennifer's. How could you have done this to me?'

Madeline. 'Hey Amy, your mum says you've not come home. Are you okay? If you want to talk I'm just a phone call away.'

Grandma. 'Amy come home. Mum is worried sick. We love you so much. Are you safe? Where are you? Please come home.'

Jennifer. 'Hi Amy. Been trying to ring you. I'm worried about you. Please come home. Give me a ring.'

Dad. 'Your tea is on the table and you're not here. Where are you?'

Daniel. 'Amy where've you gone? You told me you were going to Jennifer's. Come home. We are worried.'...
BBUUZZZZZBUUZZZZZ. My phone began to ring again. I pressed the red phone as quickly as I could; at least until I was out of the area. It kept ringing. I kept ignoring it. I began to cry. What had I done? I knew this was wrong and painful to my family, but I had no choice. The hospital was making me do this to them.

The platform started to disappear: we'd set off. The straining of the engine wheezed in my ear, and the carriage shook. 'Nothing I can do now', I thought.

The phone kept ringing and ringing and ringing. I couldn't face the sound of my parent's petrified and angry voices. It was too much. I took some notelets from my bag and started to write: 'To mummy and everyone, I am so sorry I have had to do this to you. I love you all so much, and it isn't you I'm running away from. It's the hospital and the weight they are trying to force onto me. I hate it, and will not have anymore of it. I wish I could come home, but I know I'll have to go back to the hospital. I won't come home until they agree to discharge me. Please don't worry about me. I will look after myself. I love you all. Lots and lots and lots of love from Amy. xxxxxxxxxxxx' I wrote our address on a creased envelope I'd packed and licked a stamp to place on too. That was my first port of call as soon as I arrived: to post the letter.

My phone rang again; I had to answer it. I swallowed hard and pressed the green phone.

"Amy where are you?" My mum blurted out into the phone in tears.

"I'm on the train, but I can't tell you where mummy, you'll take me back to the hospital, and I am NOT going back there EVER! I had the chance to go, so I took it. Please don't worry abou…"

"How can I not worry about you? You're my little girl and I'm not there to protect you. Is it London? Birmingham? Leeds?..." I began to choke on my tears. I was trying hard not to attract attention.

"I can't tell you. Please don't cry mummy. Please don't. I'll come home when Dr.Waissel agrees to let me go. Tell her please. I can't and won't do this." I was desperate.

"We will sort things out, just please come home first." My mum begged. But I couldn't risk it. Not now. Not ever. I had to know for sure I was going to be allowed home for good. "I'm so sorry mummy. I love you." I couldn't hold back anymore; tears began to roll down my cheeks and onto my lips." I hung up. More texts started cramming into my inbox: Sammy,

Grandma, Jennifer...Tears dripped from my cheeks onto the flowery notelets in front of me, smudging the black ink I'd scrawled on them. BUUZZZZZBBUUUZZZZZ...

"Mummy?"

"Amy, ring me when you get to the train station. I need to know you're safe." She pleaded. I agreed. I didn't like people worrying about me; especially not my family.

For the rest of the journey, I sat hunched in my seat, painfully picturing my distraught family crying at home; making phone calls; the tea my mum had made especially for me with nice things I'd eat on the plate. I fixed my wet, salty eyes on the grimy window next to me. Everything was blurred. Bushes, houses and clouds, that were blurry green shapes, brown boxes and white skies flew past me. It didn't seem real. What was I going to do when I arrived? Where would I go? I had no idea. I could feel the gathering pressure of a river about to flood from my eyes. The minute I stepped off the train and onto the strange platform, I dispensed that river.

Grey clouds accumulated and broke so the darkening blue sky could be seen: It was getting late. People carrying brief cases and handbags busy on their ways scurried past me, this way and that. Platform workers strolled up and down the platforms in their luminous yellow jackets, and a young couple perched closely together on a bench to my left. I was dazed. My tears grew heavier. I really had no idea where to head. Rusty red railings lined the platform. I raced over to them and clutched the top bar, crying over them onto the train tracks below. I rang my mum.

"I'm, here now." I just about managed to choke out.

" Where are you going to go? Please tell me where you are. I won't contact the hospital, I promise." But I was still adamant to keep that quiet. I felt a rage coming on. And I let it out...

"Oh mummy, everything is such a mess. How did my life ever get like this? What on earth ever possessed me to go to the hospital? I've never ever *ever* been so upset and depressed in my life. Please help me, mummy. Please..." I droned out into a mumble of tears and groans. My face became hot and red with frustration, and my eyes were puffy with crying. A lady approached me and asked if I was alright. Of course I wasn't! But I had to say yes and force a smile to detract attention. But nevertheless, the lady from the young couple sat to my left had approached a platform worker and notified him about me crying. He came over and asked if I was lost. I was lost, but I couldn't say that could I? But I had noticed my credit was almost gone on my phone, and I needed more to keep in contact with my mum. I asked him where the nearest shop was that would top up my phone for me. He led me to one inside the station.

Still on the phone, my mum told me to ask someone how to top it up, as I'd never done it before, and she'd ring back later. The man at the till told me to ring the number that was printed on a receipt he gave me. So as I patiently listened to the robot-like voice through my phone, the instructions it gave just didn't make sense and I lost my temper.

"Excuse me," I said to the man behind the till once I'd queued up again, "I've never topped up my phone before and I don't understand what to do. Please could you, maybe, do it for me?" I asked in my most polite and innocent way as to make him agree. He took my phone and topped it up.

Strolling through the station, people were depleting out of doors, left and right. Soon I'd be the last person there. Muffled voices echoed through speakers above, announcing departure times and destinations. It was a big station: the biggest I'd ever seen. Dim, yellow lights lit the station hall where shops were closing their squeaky shutters for the night. I thought I'd better get out of there before I looked suspicious. My mum rang.

"Did you manage to top up your phone? Are you okay? Are you around other people?" She began to cry again. "It's getting late Amy, please tell me where you are. It's not safe to be by yourself at night." As much as I wanted her there with me, I just couldn't say.

"I'll be fine mummy. I'm going out of the station to find a hotel or somewhere I can stay."

"You can't afford a hotel! " She reminded me.

"A cheap one." I added. The intercoms clashed and the voices became even more confused and I couldn't hear very well. "I'll ring you later. I love you."

"I love you too."

The sky was black by then, but there were alot of people in small gatherings outside the station. I walked towards the road, across paving stones that jutted up out of line, when my dad rang. I remember having the same conversation as with my mum: he was telling me to come home, and that running away wouldn't get me anywhere. But it ended the same; I didn't reveal my destination. I passed a row of waiting taxi cabs and crossed the road to a smart looking hotel. I needed the toilet, so I entered and picked up a leaflet about the hotel to read in the bathroom! ... I couldn't afford even one night. What was I to do? I couldn't think of anything else other than to return to the station. It was sheltered and light in there, and not quite as nippy, and there were benches too. I sat down next to a scruffy looking woman on a green bench in the middle of the hall, and took out a bottle of water, which I desperately emptied into my mouth.

I hadn't been there ten minutes, when two police officers in uniform approached me from behind and took me by surprise. One sat next to me.

"Are you Amy Lewis?" he asked. Shit! How did they find me?

"Yes, why?" I asked, frowning under the brim of my hat.

"Can you come to our office with us please?" He asked, standing up next to the other man, slightly taller and 'harder' looking than him.

"No, I don't want to." I said defiantly.

"Well you'll have to. Or we'll take you down." This was just brilliant. The plan had gone perfectly, and now this! I began to cry again and slowly got up, dragging my feet behind me as they lead me across the station, down some concrete steps and into a secret office set-back to the right. The strong smell of coffee gave me a headache as I entered a small square room, equipped with a small fold-down table overflowing with half empty biscuit packets and empty mugs of coffee, stained dark brown on the inside, a tv set high in the right hand corner blaring the Eleven o'clock news, a sideboard spilling with files and papers, and a microwave sat under the telly, its door ajar. I sat on a tall chair in the corner. A tall, jolly looking man smiled at me. I was in no mood to smile. I grimaced and looked at the floor.

"Hi, I'm Neville and I hear you're Amy. Are you alright? Would you like a drink or anything to eat?" Absolutely not! I didn't want to seem rude, but I just shook my head, keeping my eyes fixed on the dusty concrete floor. He placed the tv remote on the fold-down table next to me.

"Just flick through and see what's on." He said. I looked up.

"How did you know I was here? And how did you know my name?" I was very curious to know.

"Your dad rang us. Somehow he found out and we went looking for you." I couldn't think how they knew. Was it my phone records they'd tapped? My phone rang. It was dad.

"Amy I'm coming to get you." He said.

"What? All the way from home? How did you know where I was?"

"I'll explain later, but I'm so glad you're safe. I'll be about two hours." I couldn't believe it. The perfect get-away was foiled, but there was no way on this earth that Dr.Waissel could possibly ever let me back in the hospital now she knew just how low and depressed it was making me... That's what I thought anyway!

Whilst waiting, I texted Emily to update her on what was happening and asked her to inform the others. Two hours quickly passed when my dad appeared round the corner with a police officer. His usual jolly voice ringing through the corridor that led to the room I was at. He thanked the officers and let me to the car.

The journey home was quiet. I hardly said a word and still couldn't believe how my plan hadn't worked. But when I got home, I raced to the side of the settee my mum was sat on and knelt down bursting with tears. I hugged her tight and explained why I'd done it and how I loved her and was running away from the hospital, not home. Meanwhile my dad was in the kitchen raising his voice down the phone at a hospital worker. They'd demanded me to be brought straight back that night, but in the state that I was in, there was no chance my parents would let me out of their sight.

"How did you find out where I was?" I asked my mum through another flood of tears.

"I heard an intercom from the station when I was on the phone to you saying 'Welcome to Leeds station'." I couldn't believe it. Something that simple had ruined my chance of freedom. My mum told me to go to bed and that we'd sort things out in the morning.

"But I'm not going back." I reminded her.

The next morning, things had calmed down a little. But I was still very upset and my face was stained from the night before in tears that streaked the length of my face. As I dragged my tired feet across the hall floor and into the kitchen, I heard the faint sound of my mum's voice on the phone to who I think was the hospital.

"Ok, we will. Bye." She put the phone down. A surge of panic raged through my chest; my heart beat faster.

"I'm not going back." I was quick to say.

"I'm afraid it's against the law now you're under a section for us not to do as the doctor tells us, and she says we have to go back this morning to talk about things." My heart sank.

"But we can't. I won't. They can't make me!" I folded my arms and shook my head. But it was too late. Michael and Fay were already on their way to my house to fetch me. *My* house! Them. In *my* house! How dare they. How very *dare* they! They had no right to invade my personal space at home. Fresh tears began to trace the faded tear tracks already on my face and I clung to the radiator in the kitchen. DIIINNG DONNNNGG.

The door bell. It was them.

My mum answered the door and let Fay in whilst Michael waited in the ward car. My hands clung to the radiator tighter with each step closer she came. She rounded the corner with my mum and I threw my arms around mum.

"I don't want to go. I'm not staying. I'm coming straight back home with mummy." Fay put her hand on my shoulder and looked down at me through her half moon-shaped spectacles.

"I know you don't wan to Amy, but you have to. You have no choice."

"No. I'm, not." I reiterated.

"Come on Amy, I'm here." My mum reassured. And after five minutes of being persuaded to get in the ward car, I left the house and found myself being driven back to the hell-hole I'd escaped from.

When I arrived back at the ward, the place was scarce. It seemed as though everyone had been told to stay out of the way to give me some space. Moira had answered the door; she and Fay took me and my mum to the community room, where we waited for Dr.Waissel to join us. The atmosphere was depressing. The four plain white walls boxed us in like prisoners. That's what I was really: a prisoner. I was being kept there against my will and forced to do things I didn't want to do. The door opened and in came Dr.Waissel. She glanced at me, and through the armrest I held my mum's hand tighter, scowling through clenched teeth at the person who was responsible for all the torture I was enduring. She sat down and began to talk.

"My team and I have had a long discussion as to what happens now with Amy's care. And we have come to the conclusion that she is in dire need of help at this point more than ever, as running away has proven to us how scared of eating and weight gain she really is." I could not believe what my ears were hearing. What a load of bollocks! I mean, really, it shouts to me that it isn't the right treatment for me and I need my home in order to accept treatment and 'get better.' She went on...

"And as we can all clearly see, she is very distressed and her thoughts are all over the place. Therefore we see it necessary to put her on a one to one arms reach until we are convinced she is thinking straight and it's safe to give her some space again." I went absolutely ballistic. I was crying and wailing and pleading for them to let me go... but no. They wouldn't have any of it. And that wasn't all...

"For Amy's own safety, we have decided to remove any possible piece of equipment she could harm with from her room." This was absolute crap. Now not only did I have someone following me within twenty centimetres all day and night, I hardly had any possessions left. How was I to do my hair with someone constantly watching me? How would I hide food? How would I exercise? The nightmare just went on and on and on and on. They left the room and let me and my mum have a few minutes. And I remember as clear as crystal what I said next. "Mummy," I began slowly, "this is it isn't it. I am going to have to put the weight on to get out of here." My eyes welled up. "I want to come home, and this is the only way. I've tried everything else. I'm going to have to do it and then sort it out when I come home." My mum hugged me tight and I cried more.

I remember then sitting on my hospital bed, staring out at the magnolia tree, surrounded by Moira, Fay and other nurses as they rummaged through my belongings; removing shoe laces, pencils, sharpeners, art wire, string; anything they could get their hands on. I mean, come on, what could I have possibly done with a little shoe lace?! I felt hopeless. My life had ended. I wanted to fall asleep and never ever wake up again. That way the pain would be over.

My mum left shortly after, and I was left with Michael. That night I went to sleep. A nurse sat in an armchair inside the door, watching me. Always watching.

Every meal time proved harder and harder, and even though I knew I had to eat to get out of there, I just couldn't find the strength to do it to myself. I winced every time I imagined myself with more weight on me. I just despised it. I really did. With every weigh-in that came, my weight was creeping up and up and up. And soon it would reach the number I had dreaded to reach: 40 kilograms. Passing out of the thirties and into the forties was terrifying for me. I just couldn't do it. And that's where things started to get really hard for me.

A new patient had been admitted. We were all petrified of seeing her. A new, thinner person would make us all look overweight and fat again. Ellie had a haunting feeling that it would be Heather. Apparently Heather had been in before when Ellie had only been there for a short while. She'd heard she wasn't doing too well, and when Ellie gained a glimpse of the new girl, she screamed and ran into her room crying.

"It's her, it's her." I ran after her, but she'd slammed her door shut. I tried to talk to her through the wood, but all I could hear were muffled whines from under the covers. Megan was on that day, so I went to fetch her. She was good at calming people down.

Later on I was making friendship bracelets with Emily in the social area, whilst Max slouched in a bean bag and I was being monitored and stared at by staff, once again, when Heather was taken to her room, followed by her mum, dad and older brother. She was thin: very thin. But pretty with strawberry blonde wavy hair, pale skin speckled with freckles and crystal blue eyes. I went in to see her before bed and gave her a big hug, as I knew hugs meant a lot; especially on your first night. The next day however, would be the catalyst for yet more nasty things to come my way.

Morning came and I was up, yet again at 4am. I'd spent an agonising four and a half hours trying to do my hair in front of someone staring at me constantly, as if waiting for me to try and commit suicide. I was still in a mood and a hot sweat after going through the pain-staking OCD routine that insisted on controlling my life. At the breakfast table, Heather was not there. She was on bed rest and was not allowed to join the rest of us at the table. Ellie sat opposite me as white as a ghost; her legs trembling, a pained expression upon her face. I could tell she was thinking about Heather, and would not eat. Max, Emily and Charlie however seemed fine, as they hadn't met her before. It was lucky Sharon and Amber were on home leave, as they knew her, like Ellie.

Heather was on my mind too: what she looked like the previous night; how thin she was. I sank back into my imagination and felt again the feelings I had when I was thinner: the confidence, the pride. Now they had gone; instead lay shame, paranoia, and anger. It took me an hour to drink my fortisip, and then I was free for about another hour until the next sitting of calories! I sat on the floor with Emily, drawing a cartoon strip of characters I'd imagined up a few months before.

An alarm rang.

Nurses, left right and centre, rushed to Heather's room and the ward was filled with screams and shuffling.

Later I found out what all the commotion was about: Heather had had a tube put in, and had to be restrained. She really was finding it difficult.

For a while now I'd been debating with myself about the possibility of having a tube. It was overwhelmingly difficult to maintain the continuous weight gain. I mean, if you think about it, having a tube meant all the responsibility for the weight gain would be taken off my shoulders; I wouldn't be doing it to myself, the tube would. I knew I had to gain weight for me to be let out, but doing to it myself was just not going to happen. However, there were multiple reasons for me not to have it:

- Number 1: Weight gain would be much faster
- Number 2: I would not be allowed out of the grounds with one in
- Number 3: I would most likely be in there for longer
- Number 4: I would feel sick
- Number 5: It would hurt/feel horrid

There really was no way out.

Another Monday came. Weigh-in. 37kg. My heart plummeted through my stomach. 3 more kilograms and I'd have totally out grown the maximum acceptable weight I had imprinted in my mind. I couldn't do it. No way was I going to do it. I was healthy enough now. Why couldn't everyone just leave me alone?

Emily usually sauntered in the hall way near the kitchen around meal times, so I went to hang around there whilst I talked over my options with her; being eaves dropped by staff who were sat at arms length away.

"Emily", I whispered, "nothing I've tried has worked to get me out of here, and nothing will except for weight gain. I can't do it to myself. I think I'm going to end up with a tube!"

"It's not nice", she advised, as she had had it before, "but if you can't manage any other way, you'll have to have it. You put weight on faster with one."

I know, so everyone says…"

"And you can't hide any of it." She chipped in. She really didn't want me to get it. It would be such a set back, and would take a long time to wean myself off it. I thought for a while...

"I'm gonna have to have it." Emily gave me a big hug, and we were called to the dining room once again.

I remember the tight routines like it was yesterday, it was like a drill: 8:30am-dining room, 10:30am-dining room, 12pm-dining room, 3:30pm-dining room, 5pm-dining room, 8:30pm-dining room! It never stopped. We'd slouch in, shuffling our socked feet along the hall's cream carpet and onto the cold wooden dining room floor. Max always had his cushion in front of him. I did that at home; still do actually. I had to have something to hold, like a coat or a bag: anything. It was a shield between me and the outer world. It felt more secure that way.

I sat and stared into the thick, murky chocolate flavoured fortisip that was placed in front of me. You could see the layers separating in the cup: dark brown, dirty swirls of powder in a lighter brown, milky substance. It was disgusting! In my mind's eye, numbers were swimming in and out of each other inside the cup; each one representing calories, fat, sugar... all the nasty contents, (to me), of food. They would give me a headache. A chilly shiver prickled up my arm hairs and through my neck. There was no way on this earth I was going to let that garbage slither down my throat and land itself on my thighs. No way. The straw could nearly stand up alone it was that thick! I liked to mess with the straw and spread the drink across the sides as much as I could to save calories. Tiny drops from the end of my straw would accumulate on the sides, inching their way back towards the liquid they came from. Other than that, I had no interest in engaging with the stuff.

I sat back, slouched, and put my feet up on the chair in front of me.

"Drink Amy." Sandra demanded.
"No!"
"Drink it." She repeated.

"I said no!" She gave me a stare. I stared back. We sat there for another twenty minutes.

"Right, can you look after everything here please Shiv, whilst I go with Amy?" Sandra asked.

"Yup, sure." Shiv, (a funny nurse) replied.

Sandra picked up my cup. "Come with me." I glanced back at Emily and Ellie on my way out and rolled my eyes.

The beanbag room was quiet. Disturbingly quiet. There was just a small round table, me and the drink. And her. Budging her chair closer to mine, she picked up the drink, supporting it in her fingers, and poked it into my mouth. I pulled away.

"Amy, You're going to have to drink it, or you know what will happen." I knew too, but I wasn't going to make myself fat. She touched the straw to my lips again. I kept my mouth closed.

"I'm not a bloody baby you know!" I moved my chair away from the table and leant against the window sill, on two chair legs.

"Well, we will sit in here all day. And you are going to drink this drink." She persisted. "And when the next one comes, and the next one, you're going to drink them too."

"Oh am I? I don't think so. If I don't open my mouth, you can't make me drink it." I felt really smug.

"Then it's the tube then." She threatened. I thought for a moment.

"But if I don't let you put it in and you can't get to my nose..."

"Then we will insert it through your stomach. Trust me, there are numerous ways to do it." She finished for me. I had nothing more to say. I gave her the silent treatment.

Eventually Sandra was due on her break, so Shiv came in to take over. He was a softy. 'I could maybe grovel my way out of this one.' I thought.

He sat there. I sat there. He stared at the off-white wall. I stared out the window. I noticed he started to twiddle his thumbs. I twiddled mine. He yawned. So did I. He wasn't being much fun that day. He hadn't even clocked on I was copying him.

"So," he began, after sitting himself up out of his usual slouch, "are you going to drink it?" I liked the way he asked me, whereas Sandra just demanded.

"No." I answered. He took a breath and leant back. I was just enjoying the break from Sandra. It was peaceful with no one trying to shove a bleedin' straw down my neck!

An hour dragged by. I'd just gotten rid of my headache when Sandra swiftly opened the door and gestured to Shiv her break was over. He slouched out and she took her seat. She pulled it until she was tucked tightly against the table, and pulled out a pen and paper. She started to plan out the amount of Nutricine (equivalent to fortisip) I'd need through a tube. It was a hell of a lot!

"You still haven't started your drink yet, and it's snack in an hour." She pointed out.

"Well done Sherlock!" I felt inclined to say. But she was having no messing. She picked up the drink and pushed the straw into my mouth.

"Now drink it!"

"NO!" I retaliated. Her face came closer.

"I'll go and get the tube then." She got up out of her seat and reached for the door handle.

"NO! I'LL DRINK IT!" I picked the drink up off the table and started to suck the straw. She sat back down. The sudden thought of the tube going in was too much.

"I'll drink this one, and then that's it." I tried to compromise.

"We'll see."

Eight o'clock that night eventually crawled by, and I was still being held captive in that room. Two huge cups of fortisip were perched in front of me; their contents luke-warm and separated into powder and milk. I'd spent my day chewing the straws that sat in the cups. They looked like some mauled plastic a pit bull had got its grubby paws on! Diane opened the door, hand over had just finished and she was on nights. That made me slightly happier. I loved Diane, and I knew she'd sympathise with me. But she'd heard about everything that had gone on that day and was told that if I didn't at least drink my drink for supper, I'd have to have the tube next day.

Well, I didn't drink it: obviously. Sandra wasn't there, so I could get away with it. But I had the worst sleep I'd ever had, dreading the next day.

When I woke up my tummy was doing somersaults and my heart felt as if it was sinking deep into my chest. I couldn't consecrate on doing my best to get ready in time that morning. My head was buzzing with terrifying images of the tube. My arms shook whilst tying my hair up, and my face was white.

Breakfast came, and I was surprised they hadn't fixed one in for me yet. It turned out they'd given me another chance. Even though I was glad they hadn't, what was the point? I wasn't just going to perform a miracle and suddenly, as if by magic, drink them all up! It just meant another agonising day of torture and waiting. Ellie tried to comfort me and tried to persuade me not to have it in. But I didn't have a choice really did I? The demon inside me would no way let me sip another ml of that stuff, and I would never be allowed out of there if I didn't have the food one way or another. It was a dead end.

Later that day Shiv was doing the obs when he opened my door to check on me and I remember being perched on the end of my bed, my head in my hands; crying. He came over to me and knelt down so he was my height.

"Oh, Shiv," I began, "I'm going to have to have the tube aren't I?" I snuffled. He fixed his large brown eyes on me, and with a crinkled brow sighed heavily.

"Well... probably yes. But you can still do this. You still have time..."

"No I don't Shiv," I interrupted, "I don't. There is no choice anymore. I can't physically do it, and there's no way out of here without doing it. It's so unfair." I put my arms around him and hugged him tight. He hugged me too. "It's so unfair." I repeated.

The next day came. I was an absolute nervous wreck. I felt sick. So, so sick. I stood half hidden by my bedroom door, peering into the hall; my eyes fixed on the entrance to the ward. 8 o'clock: Sandra strode in, dead on queue. 'Great, looks as though you're definitely having it today Amy', I thought. I shut the door and paced up and down, up and down. I couldn't think. I needed a friend. I went in search of Emily, and, as usual, she was sauntering in the hall way near the kitchen area.

"Emily!" I threw my arms around her. "This is it. Where's Sandra?"

"She's in the treatment room." She told me.

"Oh no, she's getting the tube out." I hugged her; she hugged me back.

"You can do this." She offered.

The doors from the treatment room swung open. Sandra emerged holding a purple tray filled with syringes of liquid in one hand, and a long coil of tube in the other.

"Come on you." She gestured, and led me to my room. She placed the purple tray on my desk and sat on the chair, which she turned to face my bed. "Sit down then!" I reluctantly sat at the top end of my bed, hugging my teddy for comfort. She briefly told me what she was about to do, and all I kept saying was "Does it hurt? Does it hurt? Are you sure it doesn't hurt?" Her answer to this was "It will feel *uncomfortable*", which to me was a polite way of saying 'yes Amy. Yes it does.' She gave me a cup of water with a straw to help the tube down.

"Ready?"

"No!" I retaliated. She began anyway. She tipped my head back and held the tube to my face, inching it closer and closer to my left nostril. I leant back.

"Keep still or I can't do it!" She demanded. 'Exactly,' I thought! She attempted again...

"Are you absolutely certain it doesn't hurt?!" I stalled.

"Amy, come on, you can do it." After a pause I swallowed hard, clutched the furry arm of the teddy bear my mum got me when I was admitted, whilst shakily holding the water, and nodded. I inched back forward and tipped my head back. The tube came closer and closer, until I felt its cold tip touch the inside of my nose. She pushed it further and further in, until I could feel an uncomfortable scratching sensation at the top of my nostril. I had to swallow water now to help it slide down the top of my throat. I swallowed, but it didn't budge, so I swallowed harder, and I felt a stiff, thick line struggle further down my throat.

"Open your mouth so I can see it." I opened. She had to check it was in the right position. "We don't want it going into your lungs do we?!" The thought made me shiver. She kept on feeding the line further and further in; all the time a cold object slithered down the sides of my throat. Eventually she gave it a last push, and another, to make sure it was in my stomach. The feeling was terrible. "You'll get used to it." She assured. I coughed and tensed my throat to try and make the sensation more comfortable. I cried. She placed a hand into the purple tray and pulled out an empty syringe. My eyes widened.

"What's that for?" I asked in a panic. As she pulled out a piece of litmus paper, she explained, "It's to check if it's in your stomach correctly. We attach it to the end of the tube and draw stomach acid up, and test it on the paper. If the paper turns red, it's in the right place."

"What if it doesn't?"

"Then we'll have to take it out and do it again." The sound of this made more tears well up in my eyes. As she drew acid up, I could feel a horrible, warmth travel up from my stomach and out of my nose. It really wasn't pleasant. But thankfully, the paper turned red, so at least I didn't have to go through all that again. Then she gave me my 'feed'. This was Nutricine: thin, yellowy liquid in 14 separate syringes. The stuff made my stomach churn. It felt so weird: an icy cold rush spilling through me. Imagine the feeling of water going down your throat after swallowing, but having it not enter through your mouth, but through your nose instead! When she'd finished she flushed the tube with water, and I had to go and sit with the others in the dining room for supervision.

When I opened my door, I was still in shock and I felt generally unwell. Michael passed and looked at me with sympathy. My eyes felt heavy and I dragged my feet to the dining room, hunched over; hands in pockets. I felt the glare of eyes fall on me when I entered. I sat at the end of the table. I felt stupid with a silly tube up my nose, masking taped to my cheek. I just hugged my tummy and stared at the floor until the half an hour was up.

The next day, I awoke to find my tube hanging far out of my nose. I'd pulled it out whilst sleeping. Grasping the tube, I shoved it back up my nose as far as it would go, but it wouldn't go far enough. I started to panic and rushed out of my room to shout Carmina who was on that night.
"Carmina, look!" I stood there holding a long tube that started slowly slipping further out of my nose.
"Uurrgh, Amy, take it out!"
"I'm trying. What happens if I can't get it back in? Will I have to have it put in again?" I asked with uncertainty.
"Yes, I think so." She replied. So at the sound of that, I started ramming it back the way it came. But I couldn't. It had un-lodged itself. I had no choice other than to pull it out and brace myself for it to be done again.
The uncomfortable sensation lasted about a day. After that, all I could concentrate on was the sickening feeling that churned constantly in my stomach. I felt forever bloated and after every meal needed to lie down for the pain to ease. 'Is this really the best way?', I kept thinking, but when I thought of the alternative, it just had to be the only way.
Even though it felt so terrible having the tube, I, (or should I say, ED), felt very proud indeed. My tube was a physical symbol to show everyone I was ill and deserved to be a proper anorexic. Everyone except Charlie and had the tube at some time or other during their stays in hospital, so now I felt officially a part of the anorexic community; I could finally join in the conversations about having one. I was the only one at the time with a tube in. Heather had had hers removed shortly before I had mine put in, which made me feel the most ill of the ward, and so the 'better anorexic'. I felt awfully guilty though, as I'd tried to persuade and support Ellie throughout the time she had one to get rid of it, but now there I was with one myself. I know that when a person gets over having a tube and can manage without it, seeing others with one is a major set back and can make them feel incredibly sensitive and upset. I didn't want to jeopardise her recovery with

difficulties of my own, so I wrote her a little note: 'Ellie, I just want to let you know that I'm sorry for having the tube. I don't want to upset you or bring back bad memories, and if you need to talk I'm still here. Love Amy xxx'. I slipped it under her door before one of my feeds, and three minutes later I received a knock at my door and on answering it, Ellie flung her arms around me and let me know she was not upset and just wanted me to get better.

"I'll do anything to help you." She offered. I hugged her back, tight. I loved my friends in there.

Notes played a big part in recovery too. There is just something special about receiving a hand written note that has been specially written just for you. Me, Ellie, Emily and Amber slipped a few notes under each other's doors during our stay at The Priory. We did it to comfort each other. They were encouragement and friendship notes:

To Amy,

Thanks for the support, I couldn't of done it without you! You are working hard too and you deserve it! Have a good homeleave and keep up the good work! Your nearly there now!

Friends forever!

Emma.
x

To Amy,

Thankyou so much for the earings, 😊 it made me smile. Hope your feeling better within yourself and I am proud of you for trying your best to beat this eating disorder. The good days seem like a breath of fresh air but the bad days seem impossible to overcome, but thankfully there are patients here who understand the emotions. Also, I am here for you if you need reassurance, or anything. 🌸

Its hard to laugh when you cry,
Its easy to lose hope, but if you keep on smiling its certainly a start.

Happiness seems SWEET HEART far away when days are long and sad, but just as good times pass away so do all the bad.

Trouble always fades away if you can grin + bear it. But if it gets too much - call me if it does + I'll be there to share it!

From Adele xxx

To Amy,
I know your struggling but it will get better for you. Your such a great friend and you deserve better. I belive you can beet this. Keep your chin up and keep smiling I know you will get there.
You can do it :)

That night, Diane was on her shift and she'd noticed I'd had the tube put in and came into the lounge and put her arm round me.

"Oh darlin', what are we going to do with you, ey? You can do this buddy."

I woke up the next morning facing my side drawers, which had placed on the top a pale pink handmade card with a 'me to you' tatty teddy drawn on the front. It was from Diane to make me feel better. I loved it. Everyone in there at some point received a tatty teddy drawing from her. They were really well drawn and it meant so much to me that she spent time making it in her night shift, just for me. I just managed to catch her before she was leaving and I gave her huge hug.

Meanwhile, Max was having problems of his own. He would not, under any circumstance, sit down. Still. He was forever walking up and down the hallways, round his room, round the dining table. The dietician had increased his dietary intake because of it, but he still just would not preserve calories by staying static. It was rather amusing watching him actually: in his little black hat; holding a cushion in front of him, pace to and fro. I joined him a couple of times, but got warned about the increase, so stopped! He wasn't one for showing emotion, although, I was good at reading people, and I could tell something was up… banging and crashing coming from his room didn't give any signs of stress away at all!! Nurses entered to find a complete and utter bombsite. He'd thrown furniture, scratched his mirror and squirted bottles of shower gel all over the floor. I thought it was rather hilarious to be honest: first bit of entertainment we'd had in ages! The staff weren't best pleased though, and so gave him the job of mopping the floors of the ward everyday for a month. He didn't care though, it just meant burning up more unwanted calories!

After weekend passed, Kelly and Amanda were back on during the week, and when they saw me through the entrance to my bedroom with a tube up my nose, they looked rather surprised. It made me feel good though, letting them know I'm still struggling even though the weight is going up. Kelly came into my room later on in the day.

"I see you have a tube."

"Yup." I replied.

"It's not nice, is it?" She asked, as if trying to say 'told you so.' I just shook my head.

"She knelt down near my bed and put her arms around me.

"I know you can do this. You are a beautiful, talented young girl and I have every belief in you that you can beat this." As much as I'd have loved to believe her, the voice in my head just couldn't accept it. But I strained a smile and hugged her back anyway.

It was crap not being able to go out of the ward with a tube in. I needed my walks more desperately than ever now I was piling on the weight faster than ever before. But they were the rules: 'You have a tube, no leaving the ward.' What a stupid rule that was! Just because you were struggling you weren't given the privilege of fresh air. Seriously, I swear I began to wilt! I almost shrivelled to the state of my plant that sat looking rather sorry for itself in the corner of my room… not even kidding. However, I had a lot of time to sit and think about things…that was for sure. I thought so much about Miss.Elliot. I missed her and I missed the art work I should've been joining in with at college, and I missed my friends, and I just wanted to give her the biggest hug and cry. I sat in the lounge area sketching whilst texting her, and I explained the whole situation. She replied saying she'd visit very soon, which made me feel instantly a little better.

That good feeling was soon shattered by the weigh-in that followed. I'd gained 1kg in 3 days! That was just unacceptable. I was devastated by the rapid weight gain by tube. Part of me felt like collapsing in a heap on the floor and wailing, whereas another small part of me felt relieved that it was one step closer to getting out of there. I remember thinking to myself throughout my entire admission, 'Come on Amy, just play the game and you will win.' Of course I wanted to lose most of the weight when I was discharged, but I wasn't going to admit that was I?! What kept me strong was the visualisation of me being free from there and losing the weight again and being with the people who love me. I didn't want to become ill again. I just wanted to lose some of the weight so I was comfortable with myself. We all used to say this to each other to help us through, "Just play the game and you'll win." It really did help having each other by our sides. It was support no one else could give us. We were all going through the same and we weren't alone.

Even though being around friends in there was great, sometimes I liked my own company and needed time to think. Relaxing into a good painting was my way of totally forgetting about everything and being happy. Before Barry died, I'd started a watercolour scene of some boats washed up on a shore in a dark sunset, just for him, but now he couldn't have it, so I decided to do it for his family. I'd set my desk up in my room like Barry would have it in his house and paint away to loud music. It was my favourite painting I'd done, and still is to date. I put so much emotion into that picture and the effect definitely paid off. With each stroke of colour I was feeling something different: anger, frustration, despair, and when all my emotions are blended together on paper, it speaks words. It was something I was proud of, and at the time, I needed that. I was proud to be ill and thin and anorexic, and wanted to be noticed for that, but now it was being taken away from me, being proud of something was hard for me.

Sharon liked art too. She'd slouch in the lounge colouring in Disney pictures, one by one. I still have some she coloured for me. Amber was a lover of all things creative too, but she had been given a privilege we'd all have killed for. Amber had it lucky, I thought. She was allowed home for some unknown reason. She wasn't being fully discharged because she was still very ill, but she was becoming a day patient instead; only spending a couple of days a week with us. I thought that was so unfair at the time. I so wanted to be in her position.

Music was also a great way for me to forget. I'd brought my cornet with me so I could still practise for when I re-joined my bands again when I came out. It was a little nerve racking playing in there, as I didn't want anyone to hear me, so I locked myself in my bathroom and played away. I'd brought all sorts of music from band: 'Disney at The Movies', 'Oregon', 'Beauty and the Beast', all sorts. It turned out though that even through closed doors I could be heard. There was a knock one day on my door, which stopped me from playing. I opened it, and there stood Natasha. She and

Fay had been listening from their office and loved it! I blushed, but carried on playing anyway!

Distractions worked for a while, but the realisation of what was really happening to us never really went away. The feeling of depression set in all the time; even if it was only for a few minutes a day. It was always there. It was like a constant headache that lingered and taunted us. I mean, yeah the place was lovely, but when you thought about it, it was a hospital for mentally ill people and no matter how many flowers carpeted the ground, or how many bunnies roamed, nothing could hide its true colours. It was like a time capsule where the world carried on in its merry way outside the hospital's four walls, but inside, time stood dead, struggling to move on.

When the night staffs' shifts started, I'd turn all the lights off in my room and shut the door. I'd sit on my bed in the pitch black and play psp. The ball of light that came from the little screen seemed like the only ounce of happiness there was left. Being shut in the dark felt as though I wasn't really there, and everything was a bad dream. But when I got checked on every few minutes, the piercing light that seeped in off the ward shattered that fantasy.

Talking about distractions, yet another patient was about to be admitted. Her name was Nicola, and let me tell you. She was a ball of fun! It was scary, having another patient being brought in. It sort of triggered that 'comparing' we did between each other again, but having had so many people admitted after me, I was sort of getting more used to the routine now. She came for a look around, and I warmed to her straight away. She was a lively, yet, unusual character. She was about my height, was thin, pale, blonde haired, and lots of freckles lined the bridge of her nose. We all huddled in the lounge area looking at her crawl on all fours out of the beanbag room. I thought this was rather strange, but I wasn't exactly the 'average person', so I could relate to her fun personality. She gave us a dazed smile as she was lead passed us on a tour round the ward, and she jokingly hit her dad in a boxing sort of action from behind. I could tell Ellie was a bit scared, but I softly laughed to lighten the mood.

A couple of days later, she was admitted. It turned out she had been transferred from another hospital somewhere, and so wasn't new to the kind of 'programme' we followed. I'm not going to lie. I was a bit freaked out at first by her odd behaviour. It was like she didn't really know where she was. She'd do strange things like punch a wall whilst looking at the floor and talk fast to herself. Her first meal at the table was supper, and she had a bowl of cereal. She ate it fast and blurted out, "I'm hungry, can I have more?" We all stared round at each other in shock. No one EVER asked for more in there. Was she anorexic? Was she in the right place? She even licked her bowl clean after eating and suddenly jolted up right and stood up. Diane was on that night, and asked her to sit down. She didn't.

"Sit down Nicola, that's a good girl. We have to sit down for supervision in here." Nicola looked around and sat down quickly. But a second later she jolted back up again. We were all very puzzled as to what was the matter. However, after a while she sat down. On exiting the dining room, she legged it at full speed down the corridor and sprang through the window sized hole in the wall near the lounge. We all fell about in stitches, but Diane wasn't impressed!

Just before she went to bed on her first night, I knocked on her door and a member of staff who was on her 1 to 1 let me in to see her. Nicola was sat at the far end of the room playing on her laptop, 'Sims' I think it was. She seemed rather calm; a lot more so than a few hours earlier. I gave her a hug and introduced myself.

"Nice to meet you Amy, I'm Nicola", she replied in a very mature tone of voice as she hugged me back. I was surprised at how grown up and sensible she sounded. Just goes to show you can't judge a book by its cover.

Over time, the other patients and I warmed to Nicola, and we learnt loads of interesting stuff about her. She was a young journalist for a magazine and she loved to write. I had a look at some of the things she'd written and I was extremely impressed by the advanced level of grammar she used and her wide range of vocabulary. She was certainly very clever.... But why all the strange behaviour?

Not before long the alarms were ringing all the way through the wards, alerting nurses left, right and centre to dash to Nicola's room. She was having a moment again. As all the staff left to take care of the matter, we were left to hear the muffled screams and struggles coming from her room. She'd been put on a 5 to one (where she had to have 5 members of staff with her at all times.) The alarms continued to ring every half an hour during the nights, and Ellie was getting increasingly agitated by what was going on. She'd stopped eating again and became very shaky; especially when she caught sight of Nicola.

After about a week, Nicola had been from a 5 to 1 to a 1 to 1, and was allowed to eat with everyone else in the dining room again. Ellie couldn't stand her unusual behaviours at the table, and was frequently rushed out having a panic attack. I tried to console her, but she was scared stiff.

Over time though, Nicola seemed to settle in. I mean, yeah she still had a right gob on her, but she'd stopped the spur of the moment behaviours! It turned out it was all down to the medication she was on. It was sending her loopy! I much preferred her when she was a bit calmer. You could have proper conversations with her about real things.

I learnt a lot from just observing Nicola. The way she thought about food was different to everyone else. She'd gladly eat chocolate as a snack, or have crisps, which were two foods the rest of us wouldn't dare touch. However, she was quite right in her line of thinking: if she had opted against having the chocolate for a snack, she'd have had to eat a greater amount of less calorific food to supply her body with the equal amount of calories. That was a very logical way of thinking.

"I mean," She started, "I would prefer not to eat chocolate, but I'd much rather eat one chocolate bar than loads of biscuits and a yogurt and fruit." She was quite right, one of the reasons I'd gone onto the tube was because the amount of food needed to supply the amount of calories I needed was ridiculously large, and made me very bloated indeed. Before encountering Nicola and her compliance with eating things like chocolate, I'd have never associated people with anorexia with eating chocolate and high sugar/fat products. I guess it doesn't mater what the food is, unless the calories were the same at the end of the day. This still didn't make me comfortable with eating chocolate though.

    Coping with the tube proved harder and harder over time. It drained me of energy and I just felt completely ill. It gave me a pale complexion and dark eyes. The horrifying thought that tons and tons of calories and goodness-knows-what- was being forcefully pumped through my body all day was terrifying and lingered always at the back of my mind. I desperately wanted to come off the tube to slow down weight gain, but then I was faced with the prospect of eating. My plan was, that I'd continue being tube fed until I'd reached my target BMI of 18, and then I'd come off onto drinks and food, as I'd require a lot less on a maintenance diet rather than a gaining one. Plus, everyone else was continuing with home leave, and mine was stunted because of having a tube. I wanted to go home, and I could only do that if I was eating.

    Sharon told me a hilarious story that I'll never forget about what she did when she had a tube. The rules were different back when she had it. The feed was put into a bag and left to filter through the line, rather than being manually pushed through via syringe. The nurses used to fix her up to her line of feed and leave her in her room until it had finished going through. Little did they know though that every time they'd leave the room, she'd unhook the end of the line from the bag and place it into the flower pot which held a plant next to her bed. It was a genius idea! However, the plant started to show signs of foul play after a while when it grew so big. Eventually, Sharon told her mum what she'd been doing and she told the nurses. I couldn't stop laughing at this. Just the thought of an enormous flower growing out of control by her bed made me giggle in fits!

    Meanwhile, my OCD was terrible. The stress and worry to do with the fast weight gain was playing on my mind, and I kept telling myself that I was growing uglier and uglier with each ounce I put on. To combat this, I wore a hat everyday, all day and my hair never saw the light of day unless I was in bed or in the shower. I just wanted to hide away from the world so no one could see how ugly and fat I was getting.

Two weeks after getting the tube put in, I'd finally, finally reached my target BMI of 18. This was such a turning point for me. I remember the pressure on my chest lift as I saw those few magic numbers on the scales reach where they would go no higher. That was it. I'd have to gain no more weight. After weigh-in I rushed back to my room and looked in the mirror, and said to myself, "Amy girl, you've done it! And you don't look as fat as I thought you'd get!" I started to cry, and I didn't know why. I think all my emotions were just pouring out of me at once. I was the happiest I'd been in ages. I knelt down on my bed and cuddled my teddy tight, crying onto its fur. Natasha opened the door and I threw my arms around her and said with a huge smile from ear to ear, "I've done it Natasha! That's it!" I told all my friends and they were so chuffed for me. I got a few comments under the breath like, "she is no way BMI 18. Way too thin!", which made me feel even better. My first move was to ring my parents and tell them. They were so happy for me.

Even though the weight had been put on, I still had a long way to go before discharge. I still had the problem of having to go back to eating food again, and the mental side of things were no different. I needed to work hard now to be released as soon as it was physically possible, and I needed to convince the doctors that my mind-set had changed. The first step was to come off the tube. I decided to come off two days later.

The night before I came off the tube, I played one of my frequent games of black jack with a nurse from next door, 'Kylie'. She'd taught me the game a few weeks ago, and I'd really gotten the hang of it. She loved the game and always used to play it with her son. I beat her a few times too! It required a lot of concentration, and so took my mind off the uncomfortable pain the Nutricine was causing in my stomach.

The next morning came, and Moira was on shift. She led me to the treatment room to have my tube taken out. I was so scared. I couldn't stop thinking about the terrible feeling of a tube sliding up through my throat and out of my nose. Just the thought made me cringe.

"Does it hurt Emily?" I asked in a panic. I clutched her hands.

"No, honestly, it just feels weird!" She reassured. I didn't want to go in alone, so Kelly came with me and held my hand. Moira unpeeled the medical tape from my cheek and pulled it slowly out. My hand gripped Kelly's with all its might as a warm, slimy sensation slithered through my chest and out of my nose. It was all over in a matter of ten seconds. I released her hand and stared in disgust at the long, wiry tube Moira held in front of me, coated in stomach acid.

"Thank you!" I hugged them both and legged it back into my room. I stood in front of my mirror, and touched my face where the tape had been. I was me again. No more tube with a sticker attached to my face.

At first, coming off the tube and having food orally again was strange, and I would still tense my throat when swallowing, expecting a thick tube to get in the way. But the taste was so much more intense than it had been, as I hadn't tasted anything for ages. I was on drinks at first, but slowly introduced solid food again. I think me eating orally helped the other patients too. They seemed to be more determined to try and get better when they knew I was as well. Even Emily, for the very first time in two years, started to introduce solid food into her diet. I liked to think I was a good help to my friends, as they were to me.

As I'd expected, my portion sizes were much more manageable now I was on a maintenance diet. I don't think I could've gone on eating the diet I was on before without the help of the tube. I still had a fear though, of gaining more weight. It wasn't set in stone that I wouldn't still gain weight on this diet. It was all touch and go from now on, experimenting with how many calories my body now needed.

After the first two weigh-ins on the maintenance diet, I was right to be afraid of gaining more weight, as I had done. But that only meant one good thing: less food! Everything was looking up, and what was more, Ms.Elliott was coming to visit me again.

I was still in my thin summer's dressing gown and my hat when she arrived, but I didn't care, I was just happy to see her. We sat in the beanbag room and spoke about everything that had gone on. She couldn't believe so much had happened since her last visit. We talked about college and my friends, and we came up with an initial idea for my next art project when I started back in September. We came up with the idea to base my project around the theme of motion and explore the way the 'ghosts' of an object as it falls contributes the object's overall flow of movement. We decided a feather would be the perfect starting point for the project. Talking about all these exciting things that lay ahead when I came home really spurred me on to get out of there and carry on a normal life like my friends at home. I knew that would be the last time Ms.Elliott came to visit me in there, as I'd probably only have about two months left as an inpatient. She stayed for about an hour and a half, and it was such a good hour and a half too. When she left, I rushed to the dining room window to watch her car drive out of the grounds, and I thought to myself, 'that will be me leaving soon.'

It seemed everyone on the ward was making progress at the time. Even Heather had started to open up more and join us in activities outside her room. Little bits of solid foods were introduced to her too. Sharon was making progress in leaps and bounds. She had been having five-day stretches of home leave, and was shortly to be discharged. It was upsetting though, when she had her last couple of CPAs. She would shout and rant and march out of the room, followed by her mum. Apparently Dr.Waissel hadn't let her go yet, and she was so eager to just leave it all behind. Seeing the long struggle she had with her discharge didn't really set me up too well for mine. I mean, she was already ahead of me in the recovery process, and if it was taking her that long to get out of there, how long would it take me? I just kept reminding myself that everyone's situation was different, and my case might be different.

It was nice to eventually see Max take bites of solid food. It was weird at first, because I'd never seen him eat a full meal before, but I felt rather proud!

After a week on solid food again, I'd earned a weekend home, and I was absolutely over the moon. Everyone on the ward said they'd miss me so much, but I wasn't going anywhere, was I! I stood next to the community room windows and watched for my dad's car to drive down the long drive way. When I spotted our car, I opened the hatch at the top of the window and stuck my arm out as far as it would go and waved and waved. Ellie stood in my room with me whilst I packed my things, and I hugged everyone tight before leaving.

"Be good guys..... well, not too good!" I reminded them just before leaving.

I arrived home and it was brilliant just to smell the different smell from a hospital ward for a change. I gave my mum a huge, huge hug and I instinctively went outside to cuddle my guinea pigs. The feeling of being home was strange. Even though that was my home, it didn't seem like it anymore, and I couldn't wait to come home for good and get rid of that feeling. It would be my 17th birthday soon, and we always did something with the family, like go out somewhere. But this year I didn't want to be seen out. I was too ashamed of the size I'd gotten to. So we decided we'd have the family round instead.

Sunday night came faster than I'd thought, and it was time to go back to the ward again. I hated the moment I had to leave my mum. We always tried not to cry, and I never knew when the next time I'd be home again was. When my dad dropped me back off, he said the worst thing anyone could have said to the nurses, "Oh she's done really well this weekend. Eaten everything, haven't you?" I felt so awkward because he made it out as if I was fine, and I really wasn't, I was just trying to impress the nurses by complying so I could be released!

Each patient could organise to see Dr.Waissel whenever she was free, to talk about any worries we had or questions about discharge etc, and I had to put a huge act on nearing discharge.

"I truly believe I'm ready to be discharged. I'm managing everything on the ward and at home, and I don't feel as inclined to go back to how I was." This was the truth- I was complying, but not managing at all. It was painful making myself do things I didn't want to do and I desperately wanted to lose most of the weight again. As hard as I, or any of the other patients tried, you couldn't pull the wool over her eyes. She was far too well trained and had seen plenty of cases like ours' before. She'd sit and listen with a crinkled brow, and after a long pause,

"Well," she started, "you are doing a lot better than you were yes, and we're very proud of you for that. But I'm not convinced you'd stay at this weight if we were to discharge you."

"But I would!" I interrupted.

"Even so, in order for us to discharge you, you must prove to us that you can reintegrate back into college on this diet plan with no problems." The sound of this made my eyes well up. I had a calculated plan in my head about what I'd do when I was discharged, and that was to lose most of the weight before I started back at college, so no one would see me like this. Now that plan was dashed and the thought of letting everyone see me in this state really upset me. I refused. I was sticking to my guns.

"No. I'm sorry, but I won't go back to college yet. I want to be able to manage at home for a year first and then slowly get back into my college routine. It's too much in one go."

"And that's why you aren't at a stage for me to discharge you yet Amy. If I let you go now and you became very ill again, I wouldn't be doing my job would I?" 'Oh that's right', I thought, 'save the bloody skin off your own backside and make me suffer in the meantime, because that's really fair that!' I reluctantly bit my tongue and left the room. So many tormenting arguments were buzzing around in my head: if I went back to college, yeah everyone would see me like this, but nothing bad would happen, but I didn't want anyone to see me like this, but then I'd be two years behind in my education if I didn't go back this year... I couldn't think straight, so I slammed my door shut, sat on my bed and screamed as loud as I possibly could into my pillow.

Now I was back on track and earning time at home, I was allowed to take part in recreation again. It was the middle of summer and it was absolutely boiling hot, so the recreation was a trip to 'Dunham Massey' park. We were allowed to wear vest tops in that weather, so I wore my favourite flowery sleeveless vest top, with thin grey pants and some jewellery.... and my baker boy hat of course! I still loved to show off my arms because the weight hadn't seemed to have gone there, so I'd carry a basketball round the ward, spinning it round my arms and bouncing it off the walls to keep them toned. Michael and Megan took us, and this time, me, Ellie and Emily were allowed to go. We were just dead excited about walking and walking for miles round the park to burn energy! As we were about to leave the ward, Natasha's booming voice stopped us dead in our tracks.

"Sun cream, my little munchkins!" Oh bloody nora! She came up to us with a huge bottle of factor 50 and slapped it all over us. My face was white when she'd finished, much to Emily's amusement!

When we got there it was so beautiful. I'd never been before. It was a vast park with wild deer roaming about. They were so tame and looked exactly like the ginger deer with white spots I'd seen on 'Bambi'.

"Look, a goat!" Ellie blurted out, grabbing me by the shoulder, pointing ahead of her at a grey coloured deer.

"That's a deer you bloody spoon!" Me and Emily were in stitches and Megan laughed too! Deary me, I did love Ellie, she made me laugh so much with the things she'd come out with. There were so many different paths to walk along. It was brilliant. The sun was so hot, but this didn't put us off from having a good long walk. We started to slowly speed up, until Michael and Megan were small dots behind us.

"Oi, you three, stop right there!" Michael's voice echoed from about 50 feet behind us. We didn't stop though, we turned around to face them and walked back to meet them, that way we could walk that distance twice instead of once!

We eventually came to a canal where we threw bread to the ducks. Michael seemed to enjoy this so much that he didn't notice me and Ellie sneak round a corner and hide in a bush! Her giggling and rustling gave us away though! Just acting like normal teenagers having fun was such a change. When we weren't enclosed within the same four walls, everything seemed different and we could relax and forget. I remember us taking a break on a bench near some stone building in the park, and I made Megan laugh uncontrollably.

"You know," I started, "and I'm not even kidding, but, if you go to Blackburn and you didn't have a clue where you were in the world, you'd swear you were in bloody Asia!" Michael wasn't too impressed,

"Just remember where we are girls, okay." Megan sniggered under her breath, trying not to laugh too loud.

"It's true though", I muttered under my breath. Megan gave me 'the look' but sniggered again!

Kelly had switched to nights for a couple of weeks, and it was her shift that night. Sharon had returned from one of her home leaves and lay on the sofa opposite me. I was scouring the bookshelf in the lounge area for something decent to read, when I came across a cookery book. I flipped to the back and my face lit up.

"Psst, Sharon...Sharon!" I whispered. I caught her attention and she came to sit next to me.

"Look what I've found." I pointed to the page the book was open at. It was a long list of calorie contents for almost all the foods we'd been trying to figure out whilst on the ward: baked potatoes, certain types of bread; everything! I looked up and Kelly, who was sat on a chair across the room, looked at me suspiciously.

"What have you got there?" she asked.

"Nothing Kelly." We kept hold of the book.

"Give it here."

"No!" I said.

"I said give it here." I could tell she was in no mood for any messing, so I handed it over and she went to put it away in the office. I wasn't going to let her have it *that* easy!

At the dining table, Kelly gave out the suppers, which I'd chosen fortisip. She placed a pink straw into it. I couldn't help but blow bubbles. I peered at her through the corner of my eyes and she glared at me.

"No blowing bubbles." I stopped for a minute, but then carried on. The others sniggered. But Kelly took hold of my straw and leant in close to me.

"If you carry on messing around, I'll take it off you and you'll have it added to your breakfast!" It was good to be silly sometimes.

My next home leave came the weekend after, and I was so happy to be at home for my birthday. I got lots of really lovely presents from my family and friends. Two of my best friends from college, the twins Felicity and Philippa, popped round to see me in the morning too. For a moment I forgot about the hospital. Just socialising with the people I knew from my life outside there was great inspiration for me to get discharged as quick as possible, so I could hang with them again. The family came round in the afternoon and we put a bit of food out for them and we lit the cake. It was a 3D Fantasia cake. It was Mickey the sorcerer with a wand and a wizard's hat. It was wicked. I even had the courage to eat some icing.

The evening after, I returned to the ward and showed my friends what I'd got for my birthday. Kelly and Ellie came round the corner with a bag for me with presents in from everyone. They'd all been to Altrincham to buy something the day before. They'd bought me some summer Mickey mouse pyjamas from New look, and a stuffed sign to hang from my bedroom door handle that had a picture of Dumbo on saying 'Bundle of fun'. I was really touched by those. I hugged them all and I wore those pyjamas that night.

It was the 17th of August already, and college started in early September. I'd been thinking a lot about the prospect of reintegrating back into college during home leave, but I wasn't sure. I'd told Ms.Elliott on her last visit that I didn't feel ready to start back again yet, but the thought of falling so far behind; especially after everything I'd been through and still gotten this far, was too much. I just had to do it. College was so important to me and I really wanted to become successful in an art career, and putting off college again for another year wasn't going to get me to where I wanted to be.

I went into the phone room and rang Ms.Elliott. I told her I'd changed my mind and that I wanted to start that year, despite me hating my image. She sounded happy for me, but she did say not to stress if it was too difficult. I wanted to see her too. I missed her, and I missed my friends and I wanted to join in again. The next step was to tell Dr.Waissel the news. I organised an appointment to see her straight away.

"I've been thinking about going back to college in September." Her ears pricked up at this. She did look rather surprised, but glad.

"I know I'm not ecstatic about the idea," I carried on, "but I'll never get out of here and move on if I don't try." She sat forward, and I just remember thinking, 'come on Amy, you're getting out of here soon!' Hopefully this would help persuade her into thinking I was getting psychologically better. Emily was having the same problem as me. Dr.Waissel was trying to get her to go back to school on little bits of home leave, but she was adamant not to, for the same reasons as I was. I told her about my decision to go back, and she just thought I was mad! But in time I hoped she'd come to copy me and try going to school again.

We had education the morning after and we were making clay pots and containers for a summer fair we were planning to have in September sometime. I made two so I could take one home for my mum. Kneading clay was such good stress relief. I could thump it and throw bits at Ellie, and just have a really fun time. The first container I made was like a little jewellery box. It was rectangular and had a lid with a little round handle to lift it up. When it dried I painted it pastel pink with lime green dots and a ladybird on the top. The second was more of a 'spur of the moment' thing! I bashed it and moulded it into a wobbly shaped tall jar thing to put makeup brushes in or whatever. I felt really creative, so I let paint drip down from the top to the bottom. It was like something off 'Art Attack'!

Li suggested it would be a really nice idea to have a little art exhibition at the summer fair, and asked if I'd like to teach a water colour class for the patients so we could use their finished work to display. I thought that was a fab idea, and she asked for a list of things I'd need to teach them.

Meanwhile, Nicola had started acting all strange again. I think she was on new medication and it had really affected her. The ward alarms were going off every few minutes again, and nurses rushed to her room to control her. Apparently she'd hit one of the staff in one of her 'rages', and backup was needed. Natasha had taped black card to the lounge window to stop anyone being able to see into Nicola's room directly opposite. That was a temporary measure. A tinted window was soon to replace the card. We all had an idea one supper time round the dining table to get 'creative' with the window space, and everyone looked to me for inspiration. I just glanced behind me to the box of poster paints on the shelf and smiled.

After supper, I grabbed the box of brightly coloured paints from the shelf and carried it to the lounge. I placed it in the middle of the floor and picked out a lovely green coloured bottle of paint.

"Everyone duck!" I yelled as I held the bottle in front of me like a paint ball gun. Everyone screamed and ran behind the fold out doors for cover. I squeezed the bottle as hard as I could and green paint splatted all over the window.

"Mint!" Max shouted. He picked up a brown and squirted it into the green. We all dived for the box, throwing different coloured paints onto the window. Ellie raced up to the mess and placed her hands in the goo, swirling all the paint round into one huge dirty colour. The adrenaline was awesome, but I think we got slightly carried away when we threw it too hard and the walls became dripping with splattered colour!

"OOoooohh!" max shouted. We were all in fits of giggles. It was so much fun living in the same 'house' as your best friends, chucking paint all over the place at ten at night! Brenda and Rondo were on shift and when they heard all the commotion they ran in to see what was going on. Their expressions were a picture!

"Nah, nah, naah!" Rondo exclaimed, raising his hands to his head.

"Yah, yah, yaah!" Ellie answered back, giggling. Luckily Brenda saw the funny side, but made us clean up the mess with buckets of hot soapy water.

That night I lay in bed on my back, cuddling my teddy and stared into the darkness, just wondering. Lots of thoughts were buzzing through my mind, but the one feeling that had grown and developed with me through my time n hospital was the close friendships I'd made. Me and the other patients, we felt like a family now. We understood and looked out for each other. And when it seemed no one else in the whole world knew what we were going through, we had one another for comfort. I really did love them.

"So everything *does* happen for a reason." I whispered to myself, cuddling my teddy tighter. Clenching my fist, I looked up and thanked God for getting me through this; I really could sense the end of my stay coming soon.

The next morning in education, we were making more crafts to sell at the summer fair, when we all heard the news that Sharon had been discharged. We were all so relieved for her, as we knew how frustrated and upset she'd been at not achieving this over the past few months. We'd all miss her so much. She'd be back to collect her things a few days later so we could all say a proper good bye. I'd made a small cardboard box with a lid that I decorated with brightly coloured glitter and stickers. It was so much fun and such great stress relief to make something that wasn't being graded that you could just put all of your energy into and make whatever colour you wanted.

"Right, Amy," Li started, "take a look at this list and tell me what else you need for your art class this afternoon." She handed me the list. I scoured down it and everything was in place. She was going to go shopping in Altrincham to fetch the materials whilst we had dinner, so we could start in the afternoon. It was so exciting, and I wished Barry had still been there to see me taking his position as art teacher. I'd brought all his plates he'd given me especially for everyone to mix their colours on, just like he had in his house.

Just after dinner, Li came to fetch me and I set up the desks with her in education, and made sure all the right paints were out etc. When everyone came down to the education room, I let everyone pick a space and then we began.

"Right, good afternoon students!" I joked with a smile on my face. "Welcome to your first art class. I am Amy, your teacher, and today, I will be showing you through the steps to paint a pink lily." Everyone giggled. I held up a photo of a lily I'd printed out earlier and explained step by step, whilst drawing my own example, how to draw the lily. It was fun but stressful at the same time, for people were shouting out "I can't do it!" and "Amy come over here and help me!" or "Do mine for me!" all at the same time! I felt dead important for once!

After a long half an hour, everyone had managed to draw the lily, and I was very pleased with the outcomes.

"Wow, I never thought I'd be able to draw like that!" Charlie exclaimed, looking proudly at her picture.

Next came the painting. I'd provided everyone with different sized brushes and tubes of specific paints they'd need to mix the colours.

"Right everyone, listen up. I'm about to tell you how to mix and paint the background colour for the petals." Everyone fell silent and I got going.

"Now this technique is called 'wet on wet', and needs to be applied to the paper very quickly before it dries so the darker colour can spread out on top." Everyone looked petrified! It was so funny! "Don't worry," I assured, "I'll help you if you need it!" I held the example up I'd just demonstrated and everyone got going. But within the first thirty seconds, five people were screaming at me "I've done it wrong, Amy help me!" They were all doing great, well, Michael wasn't! His lily looked like a pink banana skin! I could tell Max was not in the mood to paint. He'd dipped his brush into a browny-pink colour and scribbled a spider shape over the lily he'd drawn. He folded his arms and sat back in his chair.

"I've finished!"

"Come on Max", I tried, and handed him back the paintbrush.

"I don't want to." He said. He was doing so well, but I left him to it whilst Li tried to persuade him to carry on.

At the end of the afternoon, everyone had finished their lilies and they were laid out on the floor for everyone to see. It was so nice to see them all take some pride in something they'd done, and the thought that I'd initiated that feeling was a good one to have.

Eventually, after a couple of meetings with Dr. Waissel, my first day back at college was looming, and I really didn't know what to feel.

"You're mad you!" Emily said in a giggle as I updated her on the situation.

"Why am I? I wanna get out of here, and there are no more options. It's the only way out. You should try it mate!" I patted her on the back and she laughed.

I was scared, but at the same time, unexpectedly excited. I think the prospect of seeing all my friends I'd missed so much over the months shed a little light on the situation. Even though I was looking forward to seeing Ms.Elliott again, I was dreading seeing the other teachers, as they hadn't seen me since I was on death's door. What would they say? What would they think? I knew *exactly* what they'd think, 'Oh hasn't Amy put weight on! She has a figure now.' The thought of this made me feel physically sick.

A few days later I was on a day's home leave, and my first day back at college had arrived. Everyone else had started the college year a week earlier than me, but I knew if I worked hard I'd catch up. I was shitting bricks!
'Now you've let yourself go the whole world can see it on you. You really are pathetic.'
I got up extra early just to make sure I'd be on time. The first thing I did was I ate my breakfast and packed all the food that was on my diet plan for college. It was painful having to watch myself make my dinner and pack all the biscuits and snacks in my bag, but I knew I had to do it, just for a short amount of time whilst I proved I was worthy of discharge. 'Just play the game Amy', I kept telling myself. I quickly did my hair and put a hat on, in an attempt to subconsciously cover myself up.

When I arrived at college and placed my hand on the entrance door, I felt my heart race and thump in my chest. I was so frightened. People who I recognised from before I went to hospital passed by, and I noticed them take a prolonged look at me, as if to say 'I know you...'. That was a terrible feeling. I had to rush into a toilet cubicle and lock myself in and just slumped against a wall to compose myself. It was weird standing in the same toilet cubicle I used to lock myself in when I didn't want anyone to see me eat even an apple! I took a deep breath and unlocked the door. First stop was the art department.

I climbed the flights of stairs that led to the office, and with each step I felt more and more like I was about to be sick. When I reached the top, I paused, and then I knocked on the door and peered my head round.

"Hi." I said nervously to Ms.Elliott and the other teachers in there. I felt my hands fidget under the coat I was holding in front of me, but managed a smile.

"Amy! How great to see you!" Ms.Elliott replied. I blushed.

"Well well, look who it is!" Ms.Emary, the textiles teacher exclaimed! They all had beaming smiles on their faces, and I knew why.

"Let's have a look at you then." Exclaimed Ms.Elliott. I reluctantly removed the coat from in front of my body and she looked me up and down.

"You look great."

Uurrgh, I gritted my teeth but managed a fake, "Thank you."

All day was a living nightmare. Comments like, "Oh Amy, don't you look well", "You have a lovely figure now", and "You have colour in your cheeks", really, really irritated me. I had to eat my snacks locked in a toilet cubicle, (as unhygienic as that sounds), because I just couldn't face anyone witnessing me having to eat proper food, for the thought they'd assume I was cured. There was one highlight of the day though, and that was walking back into art and everyone being so happy and surprised to see me. Ms.Elliott smiled at me and I sat down next to Sabrina. A few mutters were being exchanged and glances from across the room too, but I'd missed everyone in my class so much and it was just really lovely to see them. I'd never really spoken to Sabrina before... actually, come to think of it, I never spoke to anyone before. I was too ill and had lost my personality. I now found myself chatting to her and she was so happy to see me. She expressed her worry for me when she saw me all those months ago in the classroom. I really had no idea any of my classmates even noticed I was thin.

College days that followed became easier, and I knew the first day back would be the worst. But now that almost everyone had seen me, and nothing bad had happened, I found I wasn't as nervous being back there anymore. After a while, Emily began to slowly integrate back into school life again, and she too realised it wasn't as bad as she first thought.

So, as my home leaves became longer and I spent more and more time at college, things started to feel more normal again. In my spare time I'd keep adding to the large sheet of caricatures I'd started in the ward of the current patients and the adolescent staff. It was really funny and I only had a few more people to add. Another thing to concentrate on was the summer fair we'd all been planning. It was only a couple of days away and the finishing touches needed to be made before we held it.

Me, Ellie, Emily and Charlie went with Michael to Altrincham to buy the prizes people would win for the 'lucky dip' and other stalls too. I liked choosing the teddy that people would guess the name of. It was so cute and cuddly!

Eventually the day of the fair came, and it was to be held in a hall at the back of the hospital. We spent all morning transferring things from Education to the hall in boxes. We'd made banners which read in large painted letters, 'Summer fair' and we blue-tacked paper flags on a string we'd made around the hall too. It looked really colourful and it was great to see all our hard work finally come together. The paintings from the art class I'd taught were brought across and I stuck them to a wall in an orderly fashion for everyone to see. Max was busy with Shiv throwing mini bean bag balls at the coconuts..... apparently 'trying them out'! I helped Ellie set out the clay pots on a table near the entrance, and Emily set up the 'wack a rat' whilst Amanda organised the sweet/cake stall.

Before anyone was allowed to come in, we all had to go back up to the ward and wait for our parents to come. My parents and sister came, Max's parents turned up too, with his cute baby sister, Ellie's dad made an appearance, and patients and staff from the hospital came along as well. It was a great turn out and it was fun to do something together that made us all smile and forget about things. The highlight of the event was when the background music was stopped and people who wanted to join in with the limbo were asked to make a line. Dr.Waissel ran up in her high heels and we all burst into giggles! The music started and we all watched as Dr.Waissel impressed us all with her 'moves' as she bent backwards in her heels and made it to the other side. Ellie was hiding behind me in embarrassment as she looked on at her dad being really funny.

"Oh Daaaaaaddd!" She shouted, clinging onto the back of my shirt whilst she hid her head on my shoulder! I couldn't help myself from laughing!

In the end, we made lots of money for the 'BEAT' charity, (Beat Eating Disorders), and we'd all had a fab time. To top it all off, me and my friends were to go on home leave straight after the event. We hugged each other and we'd be reunited back together in a few days.

Eventually, after a couple more weeks at hospital and at college, my mind had started to relax a little and I craved discharge. I just wanted this all to be over now. It had been seven long months and I'd had enough. My next CPA shed light on this aspiration. The verdict was, that in a month's time, I'd be discharged. A date had been set: The 19th October. I was absolutely over the moon. I thrust myself out of my chair, flung the community room door open and raced down the corridor.

"I'M GOING TO BE DISCHARGED; I'M GOING TO BE DISCHARGED!!! They've set a date for me and everything: the 19th of October. Can you believe this??!" The smile across my face made my cheeks ache, and I just hugged everybody. They were all really pleased for me, but looked sad, as they didn't want me to leave them.

"It'll be you soon Ellie", I assured her, as I placed both hands on her shoulders. She looked hopefully into my eyes. "You too Emily." I raced around the ward and told everyone, and they were all really pleased. It wasn't often there was something to celebrate in there.

The nights I spent there soon came to as little as one or two a week; the rest were spent at home. I loved this, but I was already missing my friends so much. This just made the time I could spend with them even more special, and on my last night, we planned to turn all the lights off on the ward and tell ghost stories with a torch at the end of the corridor outside Emily's room. I'd done some research on scary stories before coming back to the ward, but I think mine was boring, as Max didn't look scared one bit! The highlight of the night though, was playing 'murderer in the dark'! We knew we could get away with playing it, as Brenda and King were looking after us that night. All the lights were turned out and we used a piece of clothing to tie round the 'victim's' head over their eyes, just to make sure they couldn't peak! I was the first one with the cloth around my head. The others spun me round and round and then distanced themselves whilst I counted to ten. It was so fun, but a bit daunting, as I didn't have a clue where I'd end up! I cautiously walked around with my arms out-stretched in front of me, and I felt something.

"Ah Ha!" I shouted. "Who was that?!" I heard manic laughing and shuffling of socked feet as they all scampered around me. We took turns being the 'victim' and it was such a lovely moment to remember. We soon got tired of using the cloth, as it was too difficult to find people, so we decided to play 'find and tag' in the dark! I was the tagger first. I counted to fifty in the social area next to the bookcase, and began my hunt to find people. I remember sneaking up to the dining room as quietly as I could and crawling on all fours between the legs of the table. Somewhere out the corner of my eye, I saw a dark figure emerge and shift to the other side. I chased the figure round the table and I soon discovered it was Max! He ran and ran at top speed down the corridor. I finally caught up and tagged him before he reached the emergency exit at the end! We had loads of really funny hiding places! Ellie was perched on top of the book shelf, as if she was planking in the dark! Brenda caught a glance and told her to get down before she broke her neck! She and I also hid together in the Staff coat cupboard. We heard creaks on the floor outside the door and then Max pushed as hard as he possibly could against the door. We shrieked and legged it out of the cupboard! I think we took it a tad too far though when I was found stuffed into the community room closet on top of bedding and boxes, as everyone was shouting and laughing and banging around, when King burst in and yelled at the top of his voice, "STOP IT. STOP IT NOW, OR I WILL REPORT YOU TO THE DAY STAFF!" I climbed out the cupboard and squealed with laughter as we all ran down the corridor. We all went to bed exhausted and full of adrenaline. I knew I'd never forget that night.

My last day. It was finally here. I never, ever, ever thought I'd live to see the day that I was free of that place. I woke up in the morning, still on a high from the night before, and I just lay on my back for a few minutes taking such a great feeling in. I thought about the past seven months and how, at that moment, I realised how much I'd been through. There'd been agony, pain, depression, helplessness, but through all of that, I'd somehow coped, as I was there, thinking back on it all. I couldn't have gotten through it without the support of my family and friends, and I looked around my room at all the cards and flowers and photographs that lined my bed board and wardrobe and just felt so grateful to have those people around me. Before getting up, I took in everything, and I still remember every detail of the room I called home for those seven months.
It was an emotional day, and I spent most of it trying to hold back the tears. I'd chosen to spend my last full day on the ward with my friends, as I'd probably never see some of them again. As hard as I tried, I couldn't keep myself from crying, and when I was in the social area, I just broke down.
"I'm sorry, I don't mean to cry, but I love you guys and I never want to say good bye." I spluttered. Ellie and Emily comforted me and Max looked a little sad too, if I do say so myself.
"It'll be ok Amy," Ellie offered, "We'll meet up when I'm free of this place too, and we can have sleep overs and go shopping and have loads of fun." Emily hugged me and that made me feel so much better.
"I wonder which one of us will be free next?" Emily thought out loud. We all conferred and our predictions did in fact eventually happen. Kelly walked passed and gave me a hug

too. Sharon had come back in the afternoon to collect the rest of her things, so that was great timing to say my good byes.

"See," said Sharon, as she stepped into my room, "I told you you could do it."

"Yeah, yeah you did. And you were right. I'm gonna miss ya mate."

"You too." We hugged and exchanged contact details and she exited my room for the last time.

Later that day, Ellie and Emily helped me pack some of my things in the bags and crates my dad had left me last time he dropped me off. There was so much stuff! I hadn't realised I'd brought half of my house with me! Going through my draws brought back memories too. I came across the stamps and notelets I'd taken with me on my escapes, and the card with the hand-made bracelet that Sharon made for me on my first night there, and the hospital leaflet I'd been handed at my assessment.

Just before tea, I took the camera I'd sneaked in out of my draw, and Ellie and Emily did the same. We decided we needed photographs of each other to keep forever, so we checked the coast was clear and ran into the community room and shut the door. We took lots of shots, but it was difficult to take pictures of three of you at once yourself! Sounds of feet came up the hall, so we stuffed our cameras in our pockets and casually walked to the lounge where we managed a couple more. Then we had to move again to the dining room as someone was coming.

At tea time I was thankful to be eating my last hard potato! The chef still hadn't learnt from my note of constructive criticism I'd sent him a few months back! I sat at the end table next to Ellie, Emily and Michael, and on the other table sat Nicola, Kelly, Heather, Charlie, Max and Amber. Nearing the end of tea, Kelly brought something wrapped up for me. I opened it at the table and it brought tears to my eyes as soon as I saw it. It was a canvas that Diane had drawn for me. It was one of her famous tatty teddies holding a flower in the centre, with everyone's kind messages of luck for the future around it. I was overwhelmed and learnt that Diane had spent the other night on her shift drawing it for me. I loved it so much and it is hanging as we speak on my wall above my bed, right here in my bedroom. There were also cards- one from everyone with kind messages in, and separate ones, along with presents from my friends, which are also hanging next to the canvas on my wall. I cried and cried after this until my eyes were red and sore, but I looked up at the wall in the corridor at the caricature I'd recently finished and laughed to myself, because I'd met such fantastic people. Me, Max, Ellie, Emily, Nicola, Amber and Heather gathered at the little hole in the wall next to the social area and exchanged contact details. I wanted to make sure I could keep in contact with everyone in there.

Eventually, Heather's parents turned up to take her home for her home leave, so I hugged her tight and we gave each other our contact info. Everyone seemed to be leaving at the same time, as it was then time for Kelly to go home, and I gave her a huge hug and I felt tears well-up in my eyes again.

"I'm going to miss you Kelly, a lot. Thank you for everything. It means so much." She gave me some kind words and hugged me back, tight. Before exiting the ward, she took one last glance at me and left. Shortly after her exit, Li came bounding up to my bedroom door with tears rolling down her face. She threw her arms round me.

"Oh Amy, I'm so happy for you, but I'll miss you so, so much." I felt so emotional it was unreal. I loved Li. She was such a bubbly, lovely person and I'll never forget her. After a few minutes, she hugged me once more and reluctantly left. I waved her good bye, and she went home too.

Ellie, Emily and I waited near the window in the dining room, watching for my dad's car to pull up the driveway. Eventually we heard a growling engine. It was my dad. My heart suddenly fell to the floor, as the realisation that this was it; I'd maybe never see my friends again, set in. We cried and hugged each other and we went to my room to collect my things. On my bed, I found a card from Moira and a card from Natasha, saying how they'll miss me and how brave I'd been over the past seven months, as they couldn't be there for my last day. It was really touching to read them, but only made my leave even more emotional.

When all my meds and belongings from the locked cupboard and the treatment room had been returned to me, I went to say my last good byes. I got hugs off everyone, and even almost got one off Max! It was so funny because as soon as I open my arms to hug him, Ellie grabbed him so he couldn't move, but he managed to dart away! I was in floods of tears. I never thought I'd be upset to leave! I entered my room, had a look around and exited for the last time. At the end of the corridor, my friends stood, watching me leave. Sadness was in Ellie's and Emily's eyes. I smiled at them whilst tears rolled down my face.

"Bye guys. I love you. Take care. You can do this… Love you." The buzzer went that unlocked the door. I took one last glance at my friends, and left.

Three years later...

10th Jan 2012

Wow! So here I am, almost exactly three years later, and I'm still writing my story! It's been a strange experience, writing this book. Sometimes I'm really in the mood to reminisce and capture every moment in words. Then others, I just can't bear to remember. I've relived what I went through countless times during the compilation of this story, and it hasn't been easy, but I want to share my experiences and let others out there who are going through similar to me know that everything will be ok, and to trust in the people who want to help you.

As soon as I was discharged, all my emotions just flooded out, because I couldn't quite absorb what had happened to me and how much I'd managed to get through. My family had organised a 'Welcome home' party for me a few days after I returned, and all my family and some friends were invited. It was like drawing a line under that bad chapter in my life and starting a fresh.

So, where am I now? Well, it's been a bumpy ride since my discharge. At first, all I could think about was losing as much weight as was humanely possible, and in the shortest time. I succeeded within the first few months, but I didn't get anywhere near as low as I was all those months ago. However since then, my priorities have changed. My A levels became my main focus, and in order to do well in those, I needed food for fuel. Attempting my best at keeping my strength up paid off in the end. I ended up receiving An A* and 2 As at A level, which I was over the moon with. Ms.Elliott has continued to provide support for me whenever I need it, and I don't even attend that college anymore. I miss her and the college so much, but we see each other now and again. I couldn't have asked for better staff and understanding from college. From the start they have just been fantastic and I'd like to thank the college and my head teacher and tutors for everything they've done for me. If it wasn't for them, I'd have never been admitted to hospital in the first place and might still be in that mess, or even worse: not here anymore. They eased all my worries with the way they handled everything, so thank you from the bottom of my heart.

Weight wise I'm the 'healthiest' I've been for a long time, which I am struggling to cope with terribly. My self-confidence, body image wise, is awful and I just hate myself most of the time. I try and restrict what I eat, just like I used to, but my body won't let me go as far anymore and I find I just have to eat when I'm hungry, as the pain is too much. Don't get me wrong, the situation is miles better than it was, and I'll even eat biscuits and a bit of chocolate every now and again, which is something. Food to me still looks like a packet labelled with numbers though, and I calorie count a lot, which drives me up the wall! I've accepted that this might never ever leave me fully, but I know there's room for improvement to make life happier for me and for the people around me.

Some people say that I love the attention of having been ill and the attention I get from the help I receive, and I can't explain how much this winds me up. I don't want attention. The last thing I want is attention and sympathy. All I want is for people to like me for me; someone other than my family to care for me; to love me; to take me in and just treat me like I'm something and look after me. I want to feel secure within my own body and not have these OCD routines ruling my life. These are a lot better by the way, and take me 2 hours at the most on a bad day. I still feel really fat if I don't get my hair right, and I still need that certain feeling for me to be able to leave it alone and carry on with something else.

Counselling has been a bit too much for me to face ever since. I've had a counsellor at college and I've been to a specialist eating disorders clinic in Salford for further treatment, but I haven't been strong enough to carry that through. To get better from an eating disorder, the person needs to want to get better, and part of me doesn't want to. I feel like if I got better I'd get fat and not care about what went into my body, which I know is wrong, but that's what is stuck in my head at the moment. Ms.Elliott shed light on this thought though, and told me to 'just do it' and to 'stop hiding from my problems and face them.'

I have just finished a one year foundation course in art and design at Manchester Metropolitan University. I really liked it there, and I loved the work I was doing. It's so relaxing when I get stuck in. Although, the same situation I had with lunch in college has repeated itself at uni. I can't eat at lunchtime when I'm in public; especially around people I know. I find it hard enough to make myself eat proper food at home, but when I'm surrounded by people it's even harder.

Also, I have just accepted a place at Edinburgh School of Art to study an Illustration degree for 3 years, and I can't wait to get started, but I am a bit scared about moving away and having to feed myself... I can't even turn on an oven for goodness sake!! I'm sure a new experience and a change will do me good though. The paintings I do in my free time are doing well. They're being displayed in two local restaurants for sale, and I've sold some and received commissions.

Since discharge I have only seen Ellie once, and that was when I travelled up to her home in Birmingham last year. We had so much fun and it was great to see each other in a normal environment and outside the hospital walls. It was weird eating together, in a house, with no staff around the table. I liked it. I think about them all every single day, and when I lay down for bed every night I read their kind messages and look at the photos me, Ellie and Emily took, which are blue-tacked to my draws. I still talk to them all, via text and Facebook, and ring up the staff at the hospital, and we will eventually meet up again in the future. Nicola was the next to be discharged after me... then Heather, then Emily, then Ellie, then Charlie, and then Max.

Most of them are doing really well, and are living a relatively normal life at home, just like me. Unfortunately, however, Charlie was re-admitted a couple of months after her discharged, as she relapsed. She has now been discharged for the second time and I just hope she doesn't fall back and have to go through all that suffering again. Amber isn't well at all. She's been in and out of inpatient care ever since and is still in hospital. She suffered a heart attack last year because of her low weight, and that really put things in perspective.

Last year sometime, as part of a project for college, I contacted the hospital and asked to display some expressive paintings I'd done around the ward. I created questionnaires for the patients to fill out too and the responses were really great. I was trying to find out what it was in 'healing art' that made the patients feel better. I also attended a few night support sessions with the current inpatients and some ex patients, and it was great to see some of the staff again, and Charlie was still in at that point too. It was hard to go back though, as I felt uncomfortable around all the ill people in there and felt the biggest since I'd already had treatment. Going back into the ward brought back memories; even the smell reminded me of the days I spent in there. My caricatures were still hung on the wall, but in a nice new frame!

My handprint on the emergency exit door wasn't there though, as it had to be removed for safety reasons and replaced with another door.... Oh well, I still had the secret one in the wardrobe!!

Music wise, it was great to go back to music centre and play in all the bands again, (minus the same problems as reintegrating back into college). I miss it now though, as you 'retire' at 18! I still help out now and again! I enjoy playing my electric and acoustic guitar in my spare time, and this really helps ease my mind when I'm having a bad day.

I guess this is where there's supposed to be an ending to the story, but I can't end it. It's an on-going journey that no one can predict an end for. I wish I could say '...and she lived happily ever after', but this is no fairy-tale. However, what I can say, for people who are reading this now and are travelling on a similar journey to mine, is that, things aren't as bad as they feel. They aren't as impossible as you imagine. The World isn't as unfair as it seems. Everything will be okay. Just trust in the people you love and live every day as if it's your last. I'd wish what I've had to go through on nobody, because it is no fun at all. But I'll always believe that everything happens for a reason, and in my case, it saved my life.

And the journey continues...

Me now.....

My website: www.amylewisart.com

To Fetter College,

Thank you for your love & support.

Love Amy Lewis.
x.

To Kathy Colleer,

Thank you for you
love & support.

Love Hannah
x